3/5/13

Sheridan,

It was nice talking to you. I hope you can get in touch with my brother, Bob.

Enjoy the read.

Con Kirkpatrick

The Party Line

Coming of Age in
Healdsburg

Shirley Morehouse Kirkpatrick
Don Kirkpatrick
Betty Kirkpatrick Vrenios
Bob Kirkpatrick

The Party Line/Coming of Age in Healdsburg: An Anthology by four Healdsburg authors
ISBN-10: 148111722X
ISBN-13: 978-1481117227
Copyright: 2013 by individual authors listed:
Robert N. Kirkpatrick
Donald L. Kirkpatrick
Shirley Morehouse Kirkpatrick
Elizabeth A. Kirkpatrick Vrenios
Edited by members of COR Creative Writing classes over the last five years.
Cover Design by Doug Fortier and Nicholas Wilson
Photos from Elizabeth Kirkpatrck Vrenios and Kirkpatrick and Morehouse family history photo albums
Printed in the United States

For more information about *The Party Line: Coming of Age in Healdsburg,* contact Don Kirkpatrick @ kirk@mcn.org (707-937-2832) POB 1155, Mendocino, CA. 95460

Dedication

This book is dedicated to the community of Healdsburg. It was a wonderful place for the four of us to spend our childhood. We honor our teachers who helped guide us through the school system. Most of them refused to accept less than we were able to offer. We thank parents, friends, and neighbors who gave advice and support as we struggled though our formative years to become who we are today.

We thank our teacher, Norma Watkins, and members of the College of the Redwoods Writing Classes for their patience in listening and making suggestions for many of the stories in this book. We are grateful to the participants of the Healdsburg Tuesday Morning Writing Project for providing us with the inspiration to patch our memories into book form.

We thank Nicholas Wilson for his artistic photograph.

Last of all we thank Doug Fortier for helping us through the maze of the publishing world. His advice was invaluable.

Forward

This book is a compilation of writings by four former residents of Healdsburg. They each experienced the Healdsburg school system and moved on to lives in the wider world.

Bob Kirkpatrick was born in Fort Bragg and became a resident of Healdsburg in 1930 at the age of one. He attended Healdsburg schools, U.C. Berkeley, and received an Ed. D. from Stanford in 1962. He served as superintendent of school systems in Los Banos, Merced, and Willits. He supervised teachers for Dominican College and taught ceramics at Mendocino College. Bob and his wife Kathleen, live on a fifteen-acre garden site in Willits, CA.

Don Kirkpatrick was born in 1931, attended Healdsburg schools, U.C. Berkeley, San Francisco State, and earned a Ph.D. from the University of Michigan in 1971. He worked in education for almost forty years as a teacher and school administrator. After fourteen years as Superintendent of the Mendocino School District, he retired and accepted a job in Saudi Arabia as Superintendent of the Saudi International School District in Dhahran.

Shirley Morehouse came to Healdsburg in 1940 when in the fourth grade. She graduated from Healdsburg High School and received an A.B. and a teaching credential from U.C. Berkeley. She taught a total of 23 years as an elementary teacher in Winters and Fort Bragg. The most exciting years of her teaching career took place in Dhahran, Saudi Arabia during the first Gulf War from 1989 through 1992.

Don and Shirley Morehouse Kirkpatrick were married in the Healdsburg Federated Church in 1953. On February 1st, 2013, they celebrated sixty years of marriage. They have lived in the Mendocino Community for the last 37 years.

Betty Kirkpatrick Vrenios was born in 1940, attended Healdsburg schools, and studied music at the University of Pacific, Northwestern, and the University of Indiana. She is Professor emeritus of vocal music from American University in Washington D.C. and is past president of the National Opera Association. She now lives in Bethesda, Maryland, but has a second home in Mendocino, CA, where she is the founder and Artistic Director of the Redwoods Opera Workshop.

Table of Contents

Ilma & Kirk

The Lattu House in Happy Valley, Albion

Ilma
1903- 1993

(Don)

My mom, Ilma, was born in the Finnish province of Karelia in 1903. Her father, Sam, and her mother, Anna, immigrated to Mendocino County in California in 1907, with Ilma and her younger brother, Onnie. The Lattu family settled first in Wendling and then in Albion where Ilma's four siblings Charlie, Ino, Mayme, and Eino were born. They lived near the old bridge in a community called Happy Valley.

Sam worked in the Albion lumber mill until 1918 when the family moved to Fort Bragg. Years later, when Ilma related the story of the family trek to Fort Bragg in a wagon, she claimed she walked the entire distance leading the family cow.

Sam's job at the mill enabled him to purchase a home on Harold Street, large enough to accommodate his family. I remember the house well because, when I was a young child, our family often drove from Healdsburg to visit. It had many bedrooms, a dining room and a parlor with a piano. Family company gathered around the table in the kitchen, which had a large pot of coffee simmering on the back burner of the wood stove. I wondered why the green wooden ceiling was covered with round marks. Later, I found out, when Eino was too slow in coming for meals, Anna grabbed a broom and whopped the ceiling. He ran down the stairs for breakfast or dinner. Those marks are still on the ceiling today.

I do not remember my grandma Anna well because I was eight when she died. I recall she had a large growth on her cheek and I wondered if all people got those when they got old. She was a strong-willed woman, who ruled the family with an iron fist. She said what was on her mind in a forceful way. My grandpa Sam was not tall but he was strong and sturdy. His broad shoulders are prominent in some early pictures. I recall his quiet unassuming manner, his broken and heavily accented English, and especially his handlebar mustache. He did the outside work and left running of the house to Anna.

The children went to the Fort Bragg schools. When Ilma graduated from high school in 1923, she went to Humboldt State Teacher's College, and became a teacher. She taught for several years before she married Louie Newton in 1927. My brother Bob was born in Fort Bragg in 1929, shortly before the family moved to Healdsburg. I was born in 1931 and my sister Elizabeth in 1940.

Ilma taught school for many years in the Healdsburg area, starting at Litton and Grant one-room country schools, where she taught eight grades, and then in the Windsor school where she was a kindergarten teacher. She was a smart and talented woman with an excellent memory. She became an avid bridge player and, at eighty-five, played in five different bridge groups. Ilma had the same iron fist quality as her mother and ran the household in a similar manner. She was not an easy woman to live with because she controlled everything in her path and when she lost her temper, she lost it violently. Although she had a good sense of humor, she had a way of alienating those people she loved most. Ilma and Newt divorced after thirty-seven years of marriage. When Ilma retired from teaching, she lived a busy and independent life in Santa Rosa until her death in 1993, at the age of ninety.

The Harold Street House in Fort Bragg

Newt, The Builder

Newt and his Ma
1896-1927

(Bob)

My father was the constant presence who made life tolerable for my brother, sister, and me. He left home at thirteen and supported himself first as a laborer on the railroad and later as a carpenter's assistant. In those days, labor must have been scarce and no-one raised questions about the age of prospective employees. He did not return to the family ranch until his father was killed in 1919. Newt didn't go to school beyond the fourth grade and, for the rest of his life felt handicapped whenever he was called upon to write. He was an avid reader and a self-educated man. Life worked for him because he was knowledgeable about the physical world and comfortable working with tools. He was creative, practical, and a tireless worker. He had an excellent reputation for getting things done. He taught those values to his two boys and later to his daughter.

*

These excerpts from old letters indicate that during his adolescence an active correspondence took place between Newt and his Ma.

6

march 17, 1910

well, I am going to go ofto workfor my self and clarnce is going with me
you had better not try to hunt me I will be all right I will be back here some day
Newton Kirkpatrick

Not only did Newt and his Ma communicate regularly but this letter dated six years later, suggests that Newt was helping out with the family finances.

Seneca feb16, 1916

Dear newtie
I seat myself to write you a few lines to let you know we are all well as common I am awful tired to night we are having fine wether now today was like a summer day the frost is going out fast well Clarie got a boy it was born 8 she has named it Robert Newton it is awful good it sleeps all the time now I had to go an stay with her Jess wouldnt try to get any one I went tuesday morning staid until Sunday eve I washed an irend monday for her an washes our own tuesday so you see I have had a hard time I was up with the baby for 8 nights it cried an it allmost got me down She will be up tomorrow there was a girl drownded in the Dismal river a week a go it was down by blacks ranch her folk live on the north side of the river she was going to her bording place she crossed all rite friday eve on ice on Sunday eve they think the horse broke thrue in a hole they found the horse but the aint found her yet I have forgot her name we never herd of them before Frank alson bought old Deb Anderson plae an andersons are gone for good we have got 3 little calfs they are nice ones the last one was Spot She give a bucket ful of milk I will sell butter now soon the ainian people is going to have a oyster super Sat at the Douglas house the wurion people bought a carload of coal they are going to get some other things wire posts an grocies they have a creamie at Freemont they clame we can sell potatose an the kind of produce we aint herd from you for nearly 3 week the last letter I wrote to you pa left it at home when he went to town an it was severl day before we got to send it. I couldn't write last week for I was with Clarie an so bisy I couldnt get to write they had a big dance at Bawldens last Sat night Mirian Got wasent hurt very bad Dicks Gotes is all well now Ray froze his feet up there it was so cold going up there the skin healed off Ray feet I am so tired I must quit write soon from ma

pa didnt go to town an this is Sunday since Elwood is here today maby I can end this with him if he goes to town an got your letter yesterday Hansoms brought the mail we was awful glad to get that check for we neaded the money thank you ever so much

from ma

In 1919 when Newt was 23, his father, Perry, was shot and killed in a dispute by Louis Holcolm who was a neighbor across the back fence. Perry, who was sixty, owned a fourteen hundred acre ranch in Hooker County, Nebraska, which he homesteaded and improved. Newt returned to the Ranch along with his older brother, Ray, to assist their mother with the details of the funeral and to help settle their father's debts. Upon Perry's death, Ray was appointed executor of the estate, and Newt's mother was obligated to sell the ranch. This sad event in Newt's life must have made him feel alone in the world but he was a good worker, capable of making his own way. In 1920 he left for Scott's Bluff, Nebraska and then to Yoder, Wyoming, Denver, Colorado, and Casper, Wyoming. In 1923 he heard about jobs connected with the lumber industry and headed off to Scotia, California where he worked in the sawmill. In 1926 he moved to Arcada where he met and married our mother, Ilma in 1927.

Newt's Ma

A Good Egg
1940-

(Betty)

My father had a unique way of looking at people and life. Because he was nonjudgmental and had a mild manner he got along with everyone. When he liked someone he would describe that person as "a good egg". Once, I heard him call a person an "Easter-egg." When I asked him why, he replied, "Because he is painted and hard boiled." There were not many he disliked except politicians, jackleg carpenters, and some radio and television personalities, who were "manure spreaders." I can't remember him calling me by my given name because he always called me "Sugarpuss" or "Sugar."

Occasionally at North Street major fights would break out between my mother and father. One evening when Mother was ironing, a battle erupted. She threatened to hit my father with the hot iron but somehow this was averted. She goaded my Dad into hitting her. I remember her saying "Go ahead, hit me" over and over, until he finally did. Then he raced out of the house to his truck and headed to his shop to sleep. Apparently this action broke Mom's eardrum and for years she harangued my father about it. I often had to minister to her ear as she lay down, pouring hydrogen peroxide into it to help soothe it, all the time she was cursing my father. Even years later when she could hear perfectly well, she complained that he broke her eardrum. After this particular fight, my father stayed away a long time. He didn't return when my birthday arrived, but when school was out that day, I found presents and a beautiful "story book" doll he left for me. I collected them and loved the sweet blonde doll with the white organdy dress and big hat. It was the most beautiful doll I had ever seen. When mother came home, I ran to her excitedly and showed her what Pop had left. She lost her temper, struck me about my head and face, and took all my toys, dolls, birthday gifts and my beautiful doll and threw them violently into the middle of the street in the rain and mud so that the traffic would run over them. It broke my heart to lose my father's gift, on my birthday.

Although he left me when things were bad, he was aware of my plight but he needed to survive as well. I went to him if I needed something and I didn't want my mother to find out. He was building a house near the elementary school and one day when I fell down and broke my thermos and knew I would get a spanking, I ran to his job site and asked him to find another thermos so Mom wouldn't be angry. I was so relieved when he came home and snuck it into my lunch box. It didn't matter that it was plaid when the first one was blue, Mom never noticed.

My father only disciplined me once. He was a gentle soul and didn't raise a hand against me. Mother was sleeping with me in my room in our double bed and I slept as close to the edge of the bed as possible to not disturb her or make her angry. One night, for some reason, I woke up in the middle of the night and mother wasn't there. I was scared and began crying. As I wandered around the house looking for her, she appeared at the door. "Go back to bed" she hissed. " I am sleeping in the other room." This upset me and I was determined to have her back in the bed with me, so I sat down at the doorway of the bedroom. When I refused to go to bed, my father got up, rolled a newspaper, and spanked me with it. It didn't hurt at all, but I remember how shocked I was that he had actually spanked me. It was one of the few times I remember my mother in bed with my father.

I didn't realize how special Pop was. He could make unique things with his hands. As a child, I had a dresser he made with a beautiful skirt around it. For my teen years, he made a shuffleboard, which was popular with my friends. When I went away to school my desk was the envy of the other girls. The music stand I adore. He fashioned it out of an old organ music rack he found in a house he was demolishing. I still cherish the jewel box with the drawer pulls fashioned out of the keys of that old organ. I thought every father could hang a picture, fix a roof, build a house, wire a lamp, lay a floor, and build a cabinet. There wasn't anything that my father couldn't fix. It seemed as if his joy was creating beautiful objects out of discarded wood and someone else's trash. He escaped to his shop to be alone and create beautiful objects. He tried to start a cabinet business when building houses became difficult. Unfortunately, he could not compete with cabinets available in the furniture stores.

My father didn't take an active part in raising me. He worked late and retired to his room or to the Masonic lodge after dinner. I knew him best when he rose in the early morning. He brought a cup of coffee to my mother in bed, and made breakfast. He would open my door and say "Time to get up Sugar-puss." I crawled out of bed in the dark, put on my clothes, and staggered down to the kitchen. Breakfast was on the table. Without fail, we had oatmeal. Once in a great while we were treated to Cream of Wheat, which was my favorite. One morning when I was old enough to be a little sassy I complained that breakfast was always oatmeal. I wanted something different for a change. Sure enough, the next morning we had something different and I found out that there was something I liked less than oatmeal - Ralston.

Small Town Memories

Small Town Memories
2010

(Don)

On one of our recent trips to Santa Rosa, Shirley and I stopped at the Healdsburg Museum, which now occupies the Carnegie Library building on the corner of Matheson and Fitch Streets. As we went upstairs into the main room of the old library, I looked at what now houses Museum artifacts and was astonished to see how small the space was. All those years ago how could the books we read have fit into such tiny shelves?

My mind's eye wandered back to the corner where Bob and I spent happy hours in the children's section listening to the Librarian read stories about Babar and his friends. Later, we read about a smart pig named Freddy, who was a great detective, *Swiss Family Robinson, Penrod,* and other wonderful books with characters who could transport our minds to distant places and times. It was the way we escaped the clutches of our mother who always knew where we were and what we were doing. Mom was aware of everything going on in town. The library was an acceptable place to hang out and Mom realized that she would find out if her two boys got out of line. Although she didn't know it, Mrs. Holmes, the librarian, was our second mother, the safe one. She was a large woman who had a way of keeping two noisy boys quiet without a yank on the ear. She made the library a comfortable place.

We took time to drive by my childhood house on 415 Grant Street and found it hidden by a dense thicket of trees and shrubbery. The house appeared the same as it did in 1941, when we moved from there to the prune ranch on West Grant Street. My father built the house when he didn't have a job during the heart of the depression. It was constructed in 1930, only a few months after the great stock market crash of 1929. Ilma and Newt were married in 1927, and my father was saddled with the responsibilities of supporting a young family. My brother Bob was a year old, and approached the toddler stage. Thinking the pastures would be greener in Sonoma County, my mother and father left Fort Bragg and moved to Healdsburg. I arrived on the scene the following year.

Since Newt did not have a job in Healdsburg, he bet against the future and went to the bank for a loan to build a house. He had only his good reputation as collateral, and Mr. Haley gambled that

Newt would pay back the money. Newt borrowed $7,000, bought a lot, and designed his home. It was small with only two bedrooms, but we lived there until I was nine years old. It took him two years to build the house and twelve to pay for it.

The Kirkpatrick House at 415 Grant Street

I had the good fortune of surviving childhood in a small town, and although my remembrances have faded considerably, a few images linger. Those memories, which are now filtered through aged eyes, seem to shake loose from my head in fragments. There was old, portly Mr. Guern, the friendly postman, who whistled through his teeth as he walked down Grant Street on his route. Mr. Guern knew the names of all the children in the neighborhood and he usually had a tootsie roll for each of us. It was a big event in our lives when the Postman delivered the mail.

In 1937, when my father was doing remodeling work at the golf course, he was asked to remove the old clubhouse. Pop seized the opportunity, brought it home in the back of his truck, and reassembled it in our back yard. This became the gathering place for our neighborhood gang. Pop cut a trap door in the floor and we dug a tunnel as an escape route in the event we were attacked by the Dickie-Stryder gang. When we had nothing else to do, Bob and I practiced parachuting off the roof of the playhouse holding an old piece of canvas, until one day our mother caught us in the act and our paratroop days were over.

I recall running after the horse-drawn ice wagon on its delivery run to replenish the iceboxes of the town. When it stopped, my brother and I hurried to the back of the wagon and were rewarded with slivers of ice. That was a treat on a hot summer day and they were free. In 1939, on Christmas Day when our family came home from a movie, our old icebox was gone and in its place was a refrigerator, which operated on electricity. It was a momentous event because our parents no longer had to buy large blocks of ice to keep our food cool. To Bob and me it meant that the ice wagon wouldn't stop at our house any more. Our mom took one look at the new refrigerator and flew into a rage. Even though it would make her life easier, she was livid because she was not included in the decision.

A small grocery store was located on College Street hill a block from our home on Grant Street. It is gone now, but I can still see Mr. Henderson as he waited on customers. He allowed the women in the neighborhood to buy groceries on credit. It was there in 1933 my five year-old brother displayed an early indication of entrepreneurial spirit. He escaped from home, walked to the store, and asked to buy a candy bar for his little brother. When the grocer asked how he was going to pay for it, Bob told him to "charge it on the books" and that is what he did. Although my father and the neighbors thought it was pretty funny, our mom was not amused about spending a precious nickel for that candy bar. She grumbled as she recorded its cost in the monthly expense book.

We drove by North Street to see the duplex Bob and I built in the summer of 1950. It was still there and I wanted to knock on the door and say "I built this duplex in the summer of 1950." but we were in a hurry and Shirley dissuaded me. We were struck by the pristine condition of the building. The lawn was well manicured, and the duplex has new siding with freshly painted trim. It looks better than when Bob and I finished it over sixty years ago.

415 Grant Street

The Katzenjammer Kids
1936-1939

(Don)

My childhood was punctuated with scars, blemishes to the body and wounds to the mind. My brother, sister, and I agree that our mother could be loving and caring, but violence lurked in her nature. Mom had a temper, which smoldered beneath the surface and erupted like a volcano when her stress level reached its limit. When that happened, an uncontrollable destructiveness exploded terrorizing everyone within earshot or reach.

My brother Bob and I no doubt contributed significantly to my mother's stress. As a rule we tried to live up to our reputation as the Katzenjammer Kids. Unlike the boys in the 1920s comic strip, we were not twins, as my brother was two years older. However, we were every bit as mischievous. My Aunt Mayme, who lived in Fort Bragg, called us Hans and Fritz because our escapades sometimes got us into deep trouble.

When I was four, our family was on a rare outing. It was a picnic at Pine Flat, near Healdsburg. We had enjoyed the afternoon in the woods and dinner over the campfire. After dinner Bob and I tore around the campground playing tag. My brother ran in circles around the campfire and I followed close behind. When he jumped over it, I followed, but slipped and fell. My left elbow still carries the brand of those embers, but what I remember most was my mother's fury as she leveled her rage at my brother. The anger consumed her. She screamed and battered her target with whatever was at hand. There was little sympathy shown for my burned arm, but retribution was wreaked upon my brother for causing me to fall into the fire. To this day, the unfair punishment my brother received seems a far worse injury than the burn on my elbow.

When I was eight, we accepted a challenge from Swede Olsen and his gang to a rubber gun war in the cemetery drainage ditch. The hostilities commenced at the appointed time and continued for several hours. The rubber gun was designed to shoot a rubber band cut out of an inner tube. It was held in place with a clothespin and when stretched, it had a range of about 50 feet. A hit was painful, but not mortal. When both sides ran out of rubber ammunition, they got carried away and the sky was filled with dirt clods. The fight got wild before it ended in a draw. Most of us took home bruises, but nobody was seriously hurt. Under a flag of truce, the two gangs agreed to renounce the use of dirt clods, but to continue the battle in a bamboo field north of the High School. The conflict took place. This time, weapons would be rubber guns and bamboo spears. Bob put together an ingenious machine gun, which could load eight rubber bands, and the increased firepower gave our gang an advantage. The battle ended when a well-aimed javelin impaled me. It struck me behind my right ear and it hurt like the devil. We didn't tell my mother what happened until two days later when the bamboo splinter abscessed and I could no longer ignore the pain. I was hauled off to the doctor's office where he removed the splinter with a scalpel. That was the easy part. Mom was steaming, and I could see there was more to come when we got home. The visit to the emergency room was painful and traumatic for me, but my brother suffered the full force of our mother's violent rage and received scars of his own. Mom's face reddened as she screamed. "You are the oldest. You're supposed to take care of your brother." Bob cowered in the corner of the room and Mom battered him with a broomstick until it broke over his back. Then, she hammered him on the head with a heavy wooden spoon. I still don't understand why Bob was punished because I got hurt. The injury behind my ear healed and remains a scar. However, the wounds in my memory fester still.

My mother's disposition never changed and she remained unpredictable throughout my childhood. My brother had a hard time being around her even as a grown man. In later years when she lived alone in Santa Rosa, Bob occasionally would drop by her house. He hoped she would not be home so he could leave vegetables from his garden on her front porch.

Don, Skippy & Bob: 1935

Bob & Don on Old Ironsides

Old Ironsides
1933

(Don)

In the spring of 1933, the U.S.S. Constitution docked at Pier 36 in San Francisco. It was a huge event and Mom saw to it that our family made the trip. Dad was between jobs and money was precious. Nevertheless, my mother purchased tickets at the reduced fare of four cents each and we boarded the special excursion train from Healdsburg. It was the most exciting adventure of my young life.

The Constitution was recommissioned on 1 July 1931, under the command of Louis J. Gulliver with a crew of sixty officers and sailors, fifteen Marines, and their mascot, a pet monkey named Rosie. *Old Ironsides* set out with much celebration and a twenty-one-gun salute. It toured ninety port cities along the Atlantic, Gulf, and Pacific coasts. The voyage began at Portsmouth, New Hampshire, a port well known from the War of 1812. She went as far north as Bar Harbor, Maine on the Atlantic coast, through the Panama Canal, and up to Bellingham, Washington, on the Pacific. The Constitution returned to her homeport of Boston in May 1934, after more than 4.6 million people had set foot on her deck.

I knew that the ship our family was talking about had something to do with the navy and that must be good because my uncle Onnie was in it. My mother did not sew often, but this time she made sailor suits for us to wear for the big event. I had a boat I played with in the bathtub, but was not prepared for the size of the sailboat we were going to see. We waited in line for a long time and finally they let us board. The members of our family were part of those millions of people.

Bob and I even got to sit on a cannon. I thought the boat would be made of metal because they called it *Old Ironsides*. I was disappointed as it was made of wood. My father said it was called *Old Ironsides* because the British cannon balls just bounced off the side of the ship. My brother was four and I was not yet two. I have an image in my mind of Bob and me sitting on a cannon on the deck. On that day, I learned how big a sailboat could be.

Old Ironsides at Pier 36 in San Francisco 1933

415 Grant Street circa 1935

Newt's Workshops
1933-46

(Bob)

Our father always had his own workshop. It was a place with room for heavy equipment as cross cut and table saws, planers, lathes, and drill presses. He delighted in making things from scraps, which might wind up in the burn pile. Newt was not comfortable with the written word and his method of expressing himself was by designing and making cabinets, furniture, picture frames, and even playhouses for his grandchildren. His workshops were his places of refuge from our Mom.

The first workshop I recall was at the Grant Street house, which Pop built in 1931. The lot, on which the house was constructed, came with an ancient garage-like structure, which served as our father's workshop. It had walls made from large stones and was probably built in the 1800s to house a horse and buggy. It had swinging doors and two dirty windows, which provided light but were too high for a six-year-old boy to see into the shop easily. It was locked when our father was working away from the house and my brother and I wondered what was in it. On the rare occasion we were asked to call Pop for dinner, we were puzzled by the mysterious machinery and wondered how it was used. One day we would find out.

I believe part of the reason our parents moved to the "Ranch" on West Grant Street, was

20

because the barn on the property was an ideal shop for Pop. It was there our tool lessons began and Pop taught us how to use a square, a level, and a table saw. In addition to our chores of tending to the garden, the prune orchard, feeding the chickens, rabbits, and milking the cow, Don and I discovered how to fix things. We learned about repairing a door on the rabbit hutch, nailing down the screen on the chicken coop, and fixing a broken window.

When Mom yelled "Get out there and fix that screen on the porch," neither Don nor I dared to argue we didn't know how. We went to Pop's shop, got some tools and figured out how to fix it. Our mother didn't tolerate anything sounding like back talk. One might say Mom taught us to use tools under duress.

Don, "Yes, Mom" (1938)

A Hike on Fitch Mountain: Don, Bob, Denton Loomis, Don Force (1939)

The Mysterious Tunnel
1935-1939

(Don)

It was spring of 1939, I was eight and my brother, was eleven. He was the leader of our pack of four, dedicated to the defense of territory from the Striders. Denton Loomis who was nine, lived a block away on Fitch Street near Hoy's Dairy and Don Force lived down the hill on Piper Street. He was almost Bob's age. Together, we wandered the Healdsburg streets and alleys of a former time. We went where older folks did not.

During the rubber gun wars that year, we discovered a large drainage ditch, which snaked through the cemetery and ended in a culvert six feet in diameter. My brother said it drained into the Russian river but no one knew where it dumped its water. It was the unexplored cave Bob had on our "to do list" when we collected matches and enough candles. The opening to that tunnel was dark and forbidding and I imagined it was home to vampire bats and other scary things. We never determined how long it was because when Mom found out about the rubber gun war, she threw a fit and said we were not to play in the cemetery again. Bob was disappointed but I was relieved.

Big Rock Candy Mountain (1939)

(Don)

A few years ago when I read Wallace Stegner's "Big Rock Candy Mountain" strong memories of my childhood washed through my mind. I was transported back to 1939. I was eight and my brother was twelve and we were lying on the floor of my aunt's bedroom in the old two-story house, which still stands on Harold Street in Fort Bragg. In front of us was my aunt's old wind up victrola getting a vigorous workout. We listened and sang along with Harry McClintock as he wailed out "Big Rock Candy Mountain" in his nasal western twang.

I was loud and sang more or less on key but my brother "couldn't carry a tune in a bucket." It was a great duet and I am sure everyone in the house and perhaps in the neighborhood could hear us quite well. The old 78 skipped and scratched through that song over and over again until Mayme couldn't stand it any more. She got even with her older sister for all the hurts of her childhood by giving the record to my brother and me. We took it home to Healdsburg and carried on with our lessons in country western. We sang that song so many times that it tattooed itself onto my brain.

Our mother was musical and we think our screeching offended her ears as well as those of the neighbors, because one day when we came home from school, we discovered that the record was broken. Mom said that she had accidentally dropped it when she was putting it away, but deep down both of us knew better. Well, you can break the record but it is hard to remove a tattoo. That tune has lived somewhere inside me for more than 65 years. And in my mind's eye I can still hear that little boy with a high-pitched voice trying to sing like Harry.

One evening as the sun went down and the jungle fires were burning,
Down the track came a hobo hiking, and he said, "Boys, I'm not turning."
"I'm heading for a land that's far away beside the crystal fountains;"
"So come with me, we'll all go and see the Big Rock Candy Mountains."

In the Big Rock Candy Mountains, there's a land that's fair and bright,
The handouts grow on bushes and you sleep out every night
Where the boxcars all are empty and the sun shines every day
Oh the birds and the bees and the cigarette trees,
The lemonade springs where the bluebird sings
In the Big Rock Candy Mountains

In the Big Rock Candy Mountains, all the cops have wooden legs
The bulldogs all have rubber teeth and the hens lay soft-boiled eggs
The farmer's trees are full of fruit and the barns are full of hay
Oh I'm bound to go where there ain't no snow
Where the rain don't fall, and the wind don't blow
In the Big Rock Candy Mountains

In the Big Rock Candy Mountains, you never change your socks

And little streams of <u>alcohol</u> come a-trickling down the rocks
The brakemen have to tip their hats and the railroad bulls are blind
There's a lake of stew and of <u>whiskey</u> too
And you can paddle all around 'em in a big canoe
In the Big Rock Candy Mountains

In the Big Rock Candy Mountains the jails are made of tin,
And you can walk right out again as soon as you are in
There ain't no short-handled shovels, no axes, saws or picks,
I'm a-goin' to stay where you sleep all day
Where they hung the jerk that invented work
In the Big Rock Candy Mountains
I'll see you all this comin' fall in the Big Rock Candy Mountain.

Bob, Mom, & Don circa 1937

Don, The Cowboy (1937)

The Allowance Dilemma
1937

(Don)

It was May 30th, 1937 and I had just turned six. Times were tough and money was hard to come by. My father had finally secured a job working for the WPA as a foreman, which was a notch above the laborers he supervised. Even though his salary wasn't much, he had a regular paycheck once a month, instead of by the job when he could find work. Two dollars a day was a good salary in that year and Ilma kept the budget under tight control. We had a garden in the back yard and when she had to buy groceries, she pinched every nickel before it was spent. One of the strong values my mother and father shared was the importance of teaching their two boys how to manage money. That year my birthday present was the announcement that I would be receiving an allowance of ten cents a week and I was ecstatic. Now, I could buy anything I wanted.

My commercial or entertainment world wasn't big in those days. Occasionally I splurged to buy a Hershey Bar, go to a Saturday afternoon matinee at the Healdsburg Theater, or own a new Big Little Book.

All the kids in my circle of friends adored those books. They were devoured until pages were loose and dog-eared, then they were traded. Big Little Books were probably the most popular items sold at the Ben Franklin Store and although it was quite a distance from our house on Grant Street, Mom permitted Bob, and me to walk downtown on Saturday afternoons to see if any new books had come in. My friend, Denton Loomis, somehow knew when a new Dick Tracy came into the store and he tried to get there first. He and his sister, Alta May, were as hooked on the books as we were. This was motivation enough for us to sweep the kitchen floor, do the dishes, get the dirty clothes deposited in the laundry room, and do whatever else Mom had on her mind. We got those chores done in a hurry. We were eager to discover if Chester Gump would find the treasure under the sea or if Buck Rogers would win the war on the Planet Venus. Scoring a new book meant dwelling in an exciting world that week.

Saturday afternoon was also the day the latest episode of Tom Mix played. It was amazing that each week's chapter ended in an exciting place and we could not wait to see what would happen next. Would the stranger from the south turn out to be friend or an enemy for Tom? Why were they posting guards around a branding pen if "there wasn't rustlers?" We couldn't wait for the next Saturday. Now that I was financially independent, I had great dreams of going to the movie <u>every</u> Saturday, buying a candy bar, <u>and</u> a new book. I was in Heaven. Then reality set in and it probably represented the first big choice in my life. Admission to the movie and a Big Little Book both cost a dime and a Hershey Bar was a nickel. If I continued to see my hero, Tom, each week, I would never buy another chocolate bar <u>or</u> a Big Little Book.

I never saw Tom again and the candy bars would have to wait a few years. Until recently our joint collection of seventy-eight worn and "dog eared" Big Little Books stared down at me from the top of the book shelves in our study. Every time I looked at them I suffered a slight twinge of guilt. Why should I have them all? Finally, one day I called Bob and arranged a day when we could divide those relics of our childhood. Now, half of the books are on his shelves and the other half resides on ours.

A Big-Little Book

Smitty
1935-63

(Don)

This picture hangs on our wall surrounded by historical ancestors. Occasionally a stranger, new to our home, asks about it. Who is this person and how does he fit into your family? Our replies do not come easily as they evoke old memories, which play a large part in the formative years for Shirley and me. Smitty was a significant influence in our young lives. We were introduced in different ways to a person who played an important role in the history of Healdsburg and whose name still graces the Smith Robinson Gymnasium.

My brother, Bob and I enjoyed living across the street from Smith Robinson because he taught us to play football and made the game real by giving us cast-off uniforms. We felt like players on the high school football team. It was in the mid-thirties and Bob was not yet ten, I was two years younger. We played football in the street and Smitty was our coach and teacher. He was like an older uncle, willing to play games with the neighborhood boys.

Jesse and Elvera Robinson and their five children came to Sonoma County in 1920. Theirs

27

was the only black family living in Healdsburg at that time, and Jesse worked as a gravedigger at the cemetery. Jesse never had much to say, but Smitty's mother Elvera, was warm and outgoing. She was a second mother to us. When our Mom lost her temper and started throwing things, we knew we could find comfort and cookies in the Robinson house.

Smitty was a star athlete at Healdsburg High in the late 1920s and received a football scholarship to U.C. Berkeley. Before he finished his freshman year, doctors discovered he had a severely damaged heart. He was given only months to live. He dropped out of the University in 1929, and went home. While waiting to die, he got a custodian job at the hospital and became assistant football coach at the high school.

During the thirties and forties, racial unrest caused tension in much of the country, but our hometown learned that behavior of one person could create positive feelings toward black families for an entire generation of Healdsburgers. Only with the passage of time does one understand the influence Smitty had upon his community.

*

When World War II broke out, Smitty wanted to do his part. He started by sending a letter once a month to every Healdsburg resident who joined the military. This task mushroomed and a committee was formed to help. Before long *Smitty's Scoop* was going to over 500 service persons a month. The ladies of the town baked cookies and cakes by the dozens. Later, during the Korean War, the commander of the 1st Battalion of the U.S. Infantry, wrote to his wife who lived in Healdsburg, and Smitty's Committee was reorganized. Our town became the first in the nation to adopt an entire battalion.

Shirley and I owe our lifelong involvement in the world of music to Smitty. In 1944, Shirley's father Harold, minister of the Healdsburg Federated Church, recognized musical talent in Smitty. Harold asked Smitty to start a youth choir and paid the tuition for him to go to choir school at the San Francisco Theological Seminary, Shirley's sister, Margy, became the organist and accompanied the anthems. Her brother, Hap, sang and played violin solos. The choir attracted other young singers and gradually became a social magnet for kids whether they could carry a tune or not. Singing on Sundays was an important part of our lives. Shirley and I sang in the choir through our high school years and when we were married four years later in 1953, Smitty arranged for the chancel choir to sing at our reception. We kept in touch with him after college and into our working years. Every time we visited Healdsburg, we would stop to see him.

In 1954 Smitty became a surprised honoree on the Ralph Edwards' TV show: *This Is Your Life*. The show awarded him a video camera, a watch, and, although he had no driver's license and couldn't drive, a new Mustang. He kept that car for some time but I don't think he ever drove it.

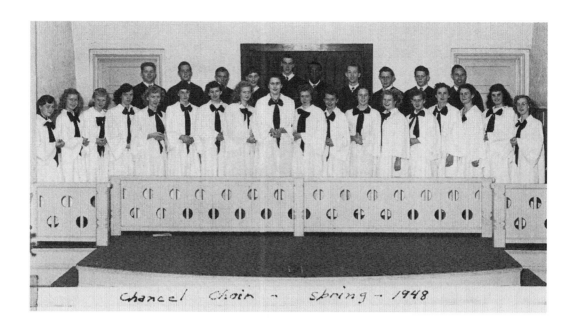

Chancel Choir — Spring — 1948

Federated Church Choir 1948

This was a letter Smitty sent to Shirley and me on February 1, 1953. It is written in ink and there were no edits or crossed out words.

Healdsburg, Caliph
Feb. 1, 1953
414 Grant St.
Dear Shirley and Don,
Today is your wedding Day – the most important day to date in your young lives. My hearty congratulations to you, and I'm so very proud of you, too. I can remember you, Kirk and your brother, Bob when you both were toddlers across the street from me. I used to give you candy and play with you.
I didn't know you quite that young, Shirley, but you were a grade school girl when I first met you, Margaret, and Happy.
Then I watched both of you grow; develop your personalities in your school activities, church life, and in choir. Your presence in the choir was always and is now, a source of happiness and appreciation for me; your sense of belonging to the group and your unselfish willingness to share your musical talents with the choir; under every circumstance, and on

every possible occasion, has endeared yourselves, and drawn you closer to my heart than you can ever realize.

I've always enjoyed your little visits in my home, whenever you come to town. In fact, I look forward to seeing you, and getting a first hand picture of all your varied activities. You really get around, and I'm most interested and deeply pleased because you want to share your lives with me.

Today, February 1, you are taking that all-important step in your lives that will mark a change from your individual living and make you a team. I've been looking forward to this day for a long time because of my friendship and love for you. I hope both of you can finish your higher education. I say this with a thought to worldwide events shaping up, and the possible disruption of college life in the event of a major war.

The choir is most happy to sing at your reception and I feel doubly honored because it is for you, and this will be the first time the chancel choir has sung for any wedding.

May God bless you richly as you start your life? He is your best friend. The latchstring is always out for you in the church, the choir, and at my house. Again, congratulations and best wishes for you always.

Affectionately,
Smith Robinson

In 1963 when Shirley and I heard that Smitty was bedfast and failing, we made a special trip from Davis to see him one last time. We choked back our tears and tried to tell him how much his friendship had meant to us. He died a few days later. Those "months" the doctors gave him to live stretched into thirty-four productive and rewarding years.

West Grant Street

1939-1945

The Prune Ranch
1939-1945

(Don)

My childhood was defined by the homes where my family lived. The strife between my mother and father ebbed and flowed with the moves. I suspect my father worked hard to get Mom to agree to a move, but when she was finally willing to go along, her stress boiled to the surface and their relationship was stretched to the breaking point. The reasons for our family moves varied with the economic times, the age of the children, and the need to keep domestic hostilities to a minimum. Only occasionally, did my mother and father agree on those reasons. They both thought that living in the country would be good for their two boys. We moved to the Prune Ranch in 1939. I was nine and my brother was twelve, and we lived there for six glorious years. Bob and I worked hard but our life there gave us room to grow. Our father and we boys loved the ranch, but our mother hated it.

The two and a half acre ranch was located about a half mile from the top of the Grant Street hill where Lou Norton's house still stands. The freeway, which bypasses Healdsburg, was completed in 1960, and built right over the site where our house stood. It survived tenuously on the flood plain west of Healdsburg for many years. The two-story house had five bedrooms, a dining room, a kitchen with pantry and porch, a living and sunroom. The rooms were large with hardwood floors. It was a house to love unless one had to keep it clean. The fact that it had only one bathroom didn't bother the males in the family, but it concerned my mother, especially after my little sister was born.

The upstairs floor had three bedrooms. Our father received a pool table in exchange for one of his jobs and it occupied the area, which separated the rooms. Our friends were there often and the place became known as the Kirkpatrick Pool Hall. When our mom wasn't paying attention, we would play games with our friends for pennies. Bob's friend, Wayne Cross, was quite a good billiards player and in 1946, the year he lived with us, neither Bob nor I ever had ready cash.

The property had a large barn, which served both as our father's shop and our hideout. We enjoyed hanging out with Dad, and the hayloft was an ideal place for Bob and me to escape from our mother. Pop, Bob, and I had pissing contests for distance out the side door of the barn. I discovered the worse you had to go, the better your chances were for winning.

We had a cow, rabbits, chickens, cats, and a dog. Bob and I divided up the chores, which included giving attention to the gardens, the orchard, and caring for the animals. Bob's job was dealing with the rabbits because I couldn't stand killing them. I was in charge of feeding the chickens and collecting the eggs. We alternated the odious task of cleaning the large chicken house every other Saturday and we took turns milking the cow. Bob did the early morning milking and I pulled the duty in the afternoon. In 1940, while others were still struggling to find work, our family luxuriated in fresh milk; butter, eggs, rabbit and chicken meat, and vegetables from our two gardens, the garden planted on top of the leach field grew like crazy. The ground was rich, a bit muddy, and the vegetables went wild. The acorn and crookneck squash produced well, and the zucchinis were large and plentiful. We gave those green monsters to everyone we knew, until kitchen doors closed with a loud "No thanks.". We were "locavores" before our time; as vegetables were served at every meal, even breakfast. During a brief window of reasonableness, Mom allowed each of us to dislike one vegetable. Bob's aversion was green beans and I hated squash. I don't know about Bob, but to this day when we go to restaurants, Shirley cleans the squash off my plate.

Earning Pocket Money
1942

(Bob)

Our allowance money came in different ways. Belinda, our Jersey cow produced more rich milk than we could use. Two days of the week, it was our job to deliver milk to Mr. and Mrs. Boucher, who lived on University Street in the middle of town. Pop made racks, which fit, on the back of our bicycles and Don and I alternated delivering the milk in mason quart jars on our way to school. Our folks paid us five cents for each one delivered. We did this until they found out that a new Government rule required all milk be pasteurized before sale. That shut down our job and half our income went down the drain.

Nevertheless, we learned there was money to be made in the milk industry and we both got jobs delivering milk for Edrington's Dairy. Their milk was pasteurized and delivered in quart milk bottles, but it meant we had to get up at 5:00 in the morning and report to the pickup station. The delivery truck kept moving down the street, while Don and I replaced the empty bottles with full ones. Occasionally, we would get a note asking for an extra pint of cream. Which meant another run to the truck. We got a lot of exercise in that job.

We also earned money by managing our two-acre prune orchard crop. The agreement with our parents was that we would do all the work relating to the orchard and get the money. This involved many different tasks from pruning the trees, which we learned from Harold Meisner, who cared for orchards, to picking the prunes, dipping them in a large washtub full of scalding lye and drying them on prune trays. If the weather looked threatening before bedtime, we spent an hour stacking the trays. We then unstacked them the next morning. It was tempting not to stack and cover the trays, but that meant we sometimes had to throw a raincoat over our pajamas and do the job in the middle of the night. When the prunes dried, we had to inspect and sack them. We then sold the dried prunes to the Coop. We never knew how much we had earned until the price was established at the end of the season. The price for dried prunes usually ranged from five to seven cents per pound, depending on the quality. We could get our entire crop into six or seven one hundred pound gunnysacks. Today, a nine-ounce package of dried prunes costs three dollars and eighty-five cents at Harvest Market.

Tomato Juice Summer
1943

(Don)

1943 was the year of our tomato juice summer. We moved to the ranch on West Grant Street in Healdsburg in 1940, the year my sister was born, and for several years, Mom was busy dealing with an active toddler. As long as we got our chores done, Bob and I were left to our own devices.

A vineyard adjacent to our house was planted in wine grapes. They tasted terrible, even when they were ripe but Bob and I discovered three Thompson Seedless vines sequestered in the midst of seven acres of sourness. Those grapes were edible, and they never had much fruit left on them at harvest time. I recall the owner discussing the matter with our mother.

We monitored the ten-acre field across the street, which had grown nothing but grass for the three years we lived at the Ranch. It was an exciting day when a tractor showed up and began to plow. The driver took a break and Bob pumped him for information, discovering that the Hunt Wesson Foods Company owned the field, and it was soon to be part of the Company's campaign to popularize tomato sauce.

The tractor returned with the trenching platform and we were allowed to ride on it and help drop the seedlings into the furrows. I couldn't believe those scrawny little plants would one day be loaded with fruit. Through spring and summer we watched them grow. It was as if we owned that field. When the smell of newly ripened tomatoes drifted across the road, the tomato juice summer began.

One night, as twilight descended, Bob and I grabbed our flashlights, sneaked over to the field. We filled a lug box, and struggled to get it home in the wheelbarrow. While Mom did errands in town the next day, we got out the big colander sieve with its wooden mallet and went to work cutting and mashing. We stashed the juice behind a curtain of milk bottles in our porch refrigerator. The next day we smacked our lips and swilled cold tomato juice until we could drink no more.

I can still taste the fresh, thick, tangy liquid we guzzled from frosty glasses. We must have harbored some guilt, because one day, when a well-dressed stranger knocked at our door, Bob and I decided that our chores were calling. Later, Mom told us that the man from the Hunt Company had dropped by to let us know we could help ourselves to all the tomatoes we wanted. We were in tomato juice heaven.

Smoking Behind the Barn
1942

(Don)

We had some freedom on the prune ranch on West Grant Street because our mom didn't venture out to the barn very often. One day Bob and I decided to see what it felt like to smoke. We didn't have any real cigarettes so we tried rolling our own with dried corn silk. That worked and it didn't taste too bad, but it wasn't like smoking *real* cigarettes.

I was a bit late coming home from school that day and my brother, Bob was already home. He had his old clothes on and was half running out to the barn. "Bob, why are you in such a hurry and where are you going?"

"I'm going out to milk the cow, and you'd better get to the chicken coop right now and make sure that place is spanking clean. Mom is really on the war path this time."

"Uuuugh, I hate that job. When I stepped in chicken poop last week, it got on the rug in our room. Mom made me wash it out, but that smell stuck around for a week. What happened this time? Why is she pissed off?"

"She didn't tell me, but I heard her talking on the phone with that nosy neighbor, Mrs. Holtz. You know how Mom is when she gets that frozen smile on her face. She told me when you came home we were to get the chores done **right now** and come into the kitchen."

"It sounds like we are in for it. You don't suppose she found out about us swimming down at Dry Creek when we were late coming home from school last week."

" I don't think so. Remember, no one was home at the Holtz place on Friday and Mrs. Holtz couldn't have seen us. Mom said something about how my shirt smelled like smoke and she was fuming. That must have been from the cigarette I found in Pop's truck last week."

"Then it must be because Mom found out about the cigarettes."

Mom made an unannounced visit to the barn and dragged us both into the kitchen by the ears. Her tone was disarmingly pleasant. "I heard you were smoking something out behind the barn. You should know you don't have to go out there to smoke. Here, sit in that chair by the sink and take one of Pop's."

We climbed up on the stool and lit up. When that one was down to the stub, she said with menace in her voice. "Here, have another one." I don't remember how many cigarettes we smoked that day but I do remember we were pretty sick. To this day neither Bob nor I ever cared much for smoking. I never forgave Mrs. Holtz for telling on us.

Learning to Drive
1943

Bob)

When I was a freshman in high school, my friend Wayne asked me to go on a double date with him. The movie we saw was "The Lady Takes a Chance" with John Wayne and Jean Arthur. It was a typical western, and Jean Arthur was charming *and* beautiful. Two tickets to that movie had cost me fifty cents. After the movie we went to Tomasco's Drug Store for a soda in Wayne's old Plymouth. They had a great soda fountain and even though they had recently raised the cost of a soda from fifteen to twenty cents, it was still the place where all the kids gathered. I knew I would have to start saving my money if I was going to do much more of this dating thing. On the way home, Wayne wanted to ride in the back seat with Bertha Deeds and I couldn't blame him. I didn't know how to drive, but Wayne and Bertha were not to be discouraged. Hannah Enzenauer and I got into the driver's seat. On the way up to Wayne's favorite parking spot, I turned the steering wheel too sharply and sideswiped another car. Pop came to get us in the Chevy and looked relieved when he saw no one was hurt. He made arrangements to pay for the repairs and took us home. The next day, Pop woke me up early and said, "Let's see how well you *can* drive. Get in and drive out to the road." Unfortunately, the driveway was a bit crooked and a big rock got in the way of the wheel. "It's time for you to learn how to drive; you can start working off that damage tomorrow." Pop said. I worked most of that year without any salary.

Mr. Aguerro Checks Out
1944

(Bob)

One of our favorite activities, especially on warm days was to ride our bikes the half mile to end of the road and jump into the deeper pools of Dry Creek, which wasn't always so dry before the Dry Creek Dam was built in the early 1950's. We sometimes would catch small trout with safety pins tied to willow sticks. The last house on the road belonged to Louis Foppiano, whose cousin owned a big winery south of Healdsburg. An old guy with long stringy hair and a straggly beard lived in the dilapidated Foppiano barn. We figured he worked as a handy man around the place and occasionally we saw him limp slowly past our house carrying a jug of wine. We found out later that his name was Lucas Aguerro and early in his life he had been a Baptist minister. We made a few futile attempts to say "hello," but learned to ignore him when our mother admonished us "Don't talk to that man." One day we heard a police car screaming down the road and we hopped on our bikes to see what the excitement was all about. We got there just before the police blocked it off. I looked through a crack in the window and saw him lying on floor. The whole place was bloody and it smelled awful. Later we heard that Mr. Aguerro had put a gun in his mouth and scattered his brains all over the room. We both felt sick when we saw blood and gore spattered all over the inside wall of the barn. Apparently, he had no relatives and we never found out why he killed himself.

The Fire Balloons
1944

(Don)

In 1944, we heard that the Japanese were launching fire balloons designed to incinerate the western United States. I imagine this panicked most parents, but as a thirteen-year-old boy, I was intrigued by the possibility of being the first to spy a huge balloon sailing overhead. We scanned the sky for weeks, especially on stormy days when we would imagine every misshapen cloud to be loaded with an incendiary device. Later that year, however, a P-38 from the US Air Force crashed into the top of Fitch Mountain and caused pandemonium in the town. Some of the high school kids cut school and got to the crash site before the Air Force was able to cordon it off. They collected twisted aluminum souvenirs and sold them for high prices. Rumors about body parts being scattered all over the mountain were finally put to rest when we heard that the pilot had bailed out before the crash occurred. This was heady stuff for young boys and our imaginations went wild.

Mr. Holtz who lived a quarter mile down the street was grouchy when kids were around. He spoke with a heavy German accent and repaired radios. That combination was sufficient to convince Bob and me he was a German spy conveying important secrets to the homeland. Bob called our gang together to do our part for the war effort. We tried to figure out a way to catch him in the act, but our efforts were in vain. I could never understand why Mr. Holtz would be spying in Healdsburg and what kind of information he'd send to Germany anyway.

The Floods
1944

(Don)

Bob and I enjoyed living at the Prune ranch because it was exciting when the small creek, which normally meandered through the valley, overflowed its banks and flooded our ranch. We swam well enough that our parents didn't worry for our safety, and Pop built a kayak, which got plenty of use in the wet years.

One day in 1944 when Bob was a sophomore, Mr. Parsons called him out of class, "Your mother just called and said for you to go home, get the cow out of the barn, and take it to the top of the hill where Mr. Norton will let you stake it in his lot until the flood waters go down."

Lou Norton owned the large house at the corner of West Grant and Grove Streets as well as a lot across the street. Belinda stayed in his field for a week and Bob and I took turns hiking up the hill to milk her. Carrying that bucketful of milk back home was not easy.

(Bob)

That year was an unusually wet one and after one heavy storm, the water was waist deep in our yard. Gradually it rose to the top step of the porch. Don and I had no trouble wading out to the barn until the water rose to our armpits. The chicken house was set far enough above the ground so that the perches and the laying nests were dry. Our rabbit population was down at that time and I could get them all in the top cages of the hutch. The rabbits and Chickens survived the flood well. Mom was beside herself as she stuffed towels and rags under the door to keep the rising water from getting into the house. It flowed over the last step onto the porch, but never reached the door. I heard my mother say, "That does it. As soon as we sell this place, we are moving back to town."

(Betty)

Occasionally in the winter, the rains would be so hard that the back yard would become a brown lake that slowly rose until it stopped at the steps to the house. While my father donned hip boots, my brothers would row to the barn in order milk the cow and feed the other animals. I would beg to go and finally after much pleading, was rewarded with a ride to the barn in the wobbly boat. I could hardly contain my delight as I saw the world from a totally different view. The yard was now a magical lake. The plants and road were gone and the trees seemed ill at ease with their feet stuck in the mud – holding their leafy skirts high.

Kayaking on Dry Creek

There is No Santa
1945

(Don)

The Christmas of 1945, my little sister discovered there was no Santa Claus. I was fourteen and Betty was five. My older brother Bob and I teased our sister unmercifully, but even at her age she handled it well. My mother, who was teaching in Windsor, borrowed a Santa Claus suit and the only question was, who would play Santa Claus? We flipped a coin and I lost. The Christmas tree was decorated and the presents were under it. Pop, Mom, Bob, and Betty had arrived in the living room and were looking through the gifts when I opened the door loaded with my sack and yelled "*Merry Christmas*" Betty's mouth opened wide. The silence was broken by Bob's mutter. "Hey, that's my pillowcase." At that moment Betty discovered the real world. To this day she relates this story of where and when she found out there is no Santa Claus.

A Memorable Christmas
1944

(Betty)

I had a pillow I carried around with me and loved to feel the velvety texture against my cheek. It was especially wonderful when it had been close to the fire and was toasty warm. I would lay it next to the heater to get it warm, and then lie down on it, sucking my thumb in great comfort. One Christmas I left the pillow too long on the heater, and it began to singe. With fear, I turned the burnt side over to hide it so that I wouldn't get spanked. I sat next to my brother Bob staring up at the Christmas tree which was brightly lit. Suddenly there was a sound at the window and Bob whispered excitedly, "There's Santa Claus. Look, he's coming." I looked up, and sure enough, a red and white apparition was crawling in the window carrying a big white sack that bulged with presents.

Bob murmured something about his pillowcase and laughed. I immediately knew that Santa was my brother, Don. I decided to play along with my two big brothers in this wonderful game as Santa tried to lower his voice with "Ho, ho, ho, Here's a present for you, little girl." After handing out the presents, he disappeared through the window and I knew at that moment that Santa was a myth.

Memories of West Grant Street
1943-44

(Betty)

Such sensations: the cold dewy surface of the white wooden lawn chair- so big that when I crawled into it, the sloped back seat would not release me from its jaws; my green itchy wool sweater and the front of my dress wet from the dew. The morning, exciting in the promise of adventure, smilingly offers me the golden coins of time with outstretched hands. My mind teems with the exciting prospects of kittens, crickets and worms. I place my mud pies with great anticipation in the makeshift oven of upturned prune boxes. "What a present it will be for my "Pop" when he comes home from work and sweeps me up in his arms with a 'Hello Sugarpuss. "

The smells: Hay from the barn – baked in the sun, the milk tasting of hay. The dark shadows in the barn cooled me as I looked upward at the eves at the sunlight lit by the dust motes, which disappeared into the darkness far above my head. I felt the excitement of looking for a warm egg hidden in magical places – a prize to be discovered and carried proudly to mother who would carefully place it in our icebox in the cavernous kitchen.

I spent endless afternoons playing in the sun, discovering the magical scents of flowers or tasty parsley growing in the shade of the tank house. I tasted the sharp pungent green of the guavas strewn over the cement path and scooped piles of fallen camellias to make houses. The tall palms in the front yard filled me with awe as I lay on the grass and peeked through the branches trying to find shapes in the cloudy sky.

I shivered if I remained too long on the east side of the house. There were times when sitting in the cold shadows, my legs and seat would become numb from the cement, for I feared the voice which would call me from the back door and draw me inside. The fear of violence rendered me motionless. I was afraid to run and play, but rather drew myself into a ball, hoping if I remained still enough, mother's anger would subside.

The Missing Bird
1943

(Betty)

When I was two and a half, I caught a bird with a damaged wing in the front yard of the house. I brought it inside, gingerly carrying it and demanded we take care of it. Tenderly I placed it in a spare cage we found in the attic and watched over its little brown body, trying to feed it for several days. One afternoon when I got up from my nap, I discovered that I was alone in the house. I ran from room to room and discovered not only my mother wasn't there, but also my bird was gone. I wept and screamed in fear and apprehension. Finally mother drove up "Sweat did you do with my bbbird?" I hiccupped.

"I let him go into the wild." Panicked, I imagined all sorts of terrible things happening to the bird and ran to the front yard to look for him. He was nowhere to be found.

"Where did you go and why did you leave me? " I sobbed, feeling desolate about the bird. Showing me a piece of paper, Mother laughed, "I left you a note where I was going." I looked at the piece of paper with total incomprehension. "But I can't read."

"Look what I got for you in town while you were asleep. It says on the note." From the back seat of the car she pulled a cage containing a beautiful golden canary. It took a lot to calm me down, but I fell in love with that bird. That day, I resolved to learn to read, and quickly.

Picking Parsley

(Betty)

We lived in many different houses during our childhood. I was born while the family was living on West Grant Street in a big two-story house with a barn full of rabbits and chickens. I loved the strawberry patch next to the driveway and I would often peer through the leaves for the succulent heaven found in the small red berries. Two huge camellia bushes (To me they were trees.) flanked the front door and at times you had to pick your way through the striped pink blossoms to walk up the steps and enter the front screen door. During parts of the year I could pick up pineapple guavas off the sidewalk on the west side of the house. I loved the sweet pungent odor and taste that simultaneously would pucker my mouth and tickle my nose. Morning glories also grew on that dark side of the house in the small field, and some mornings I would find them wet with dew that would soak the entire front of my dress as I rolled in the glorious blue field. I was well acquainted with the small parsley patch growing against the wall of the pump house, for picking the parsley was one of my "chores" for dinner preparation.

Poked by the Cow

(Betty)

I was too small to take part in the regular chores and work as my brothers and father did. I loved the dark cool interior of the old barn where I could jump into a stack of gunny sacks, the *hempy* smell filling my nostrils and the rising dust motes coloring the one rare beam of light spiking its way in through the hole in the western wall. One side of the barn opened into the pen where we kept our cow - a large leggy creature, which I managed to annoy. My brothers and father would milk the cow, sitting on a three-legged stool squirting fresh aromatic milk into the metal bucket and occasionally into our barn cat. Try as I could, my little hands couldn't tease the liquid from the bloated udder. I loved following my Pop and brothers when they worked outside. One evening when Pop went into the pen to bring the cow into the barn, I slipped through the rough fence and ran toward him. Pop was on the other side of the pen between the cow and me. "Look out" he yelled when he saw me coming in the pen. He came after me but too late. The cow saw me and trotted after the interloper. She caught me with one horn in the middle of my forehead. I carry the scar there to this day

Betty's Tea Parties (1944)

(Betty)

The small patch of grass in the back yard hosted tea parties. My playmate and I were allowed to explore a big box of discarded clothes and shoes in the closet and once we chose, we clunked down the little path, tripping over the long dresses, to the small table and chairs in which sat Nina, my rag doll, whose face was green from a crayola goblin mask for Halloween. We had tea (usually in the form of lemonade), drinking from the tiny painted tin cups and saucers and eating cookies purloined from the kitchen.

In the back yard we had a large ancient fig tree, which offered fruit if you climbed high in the sturdy branches. I loved being in the trees and would climb any if given a chance. I could not believe how my older brothers could climb trees and poles I couldn't master. One of my favorite memories was taking a nap in a hammock strung between two blooming prune trees. I coaxed my father and brothers to hoist it as high as they could so I could fall asleep in the middle of the blossoms. I was in a fairyland, the princess in her magic boat floating over a blossom sea, like the owl and the pussycat did.

The Tea Party (1944)
(Don)

The ranch is gone now. My parents were forced to sell the property to the State to make way for the new freeway built in the 1950s. When we head south on Highway 101, I count thirty seconds after we pass the Alexander Valley turn off at Healdsburg and observe: "We just drove over our old house." As I do, all those images of our childhood days on West Grant Street come flooding again into my mind.

Don, Newt, Bob in 37' Chevy

The Trip to Nebraska
1941

(Don)

It was the summer of 1941 and our sister, Betty, was a year old, Bob was twelve, and I had turned ten. Our mom was not making life pleasant around the farm. Pop heard that his older sister, Alice, had suffered a stroke, was bedfast and not expected to live long. Pop hadn't been to the Midwest for fourteen years, and it was past time for a visit. He and Mom had some heated discussions over the trip and she adamantly refused to travel with a baby. Pop stayed with the decision, packed his two boys into the 37 Chevy and we headed for Nebraska.

Newt's sister was seventeen years older than he and was largely responsible for raising him. Newt knew this would be his last opportunity to say good-bye to his sister. I think he also wanted to show off his boys to relatives, and the trip would give him at least a short respite from familial contentiousness at home.

Along the way we stopped to see the Hill family in Wyoming and various relatives in Nebraska. We spent some time visiting with Alice. The records show that she was born in 1882 and died in 1942. When we saw her, she appeared old and emaciated. Bob and I couldn't relate to anything she said. It seemed the whole town was there, but it turned out they were mostly relatives.

Kirkpatrick Relatives in Wyoming (1941)

Kirkpatrick Relatives in Nebraska (1930)

44

The Fairy Shoes
1943

(Betty)

To speak of my mother is unspeakably difficult, for it requires putting on paper shadows, fears, and anger - all difficult to pull from the ethers. The memories snake backwards so far into the distance that I cannot see past the curve of them. With luck, I may never recall all the atrocities that stretch like a tail into the black hole of memory. Instead, I start at the first of my memories - the beginning - shoes.

These were not just any shoes, but sweet, black, licorice shiny, paten-leather shoes with the softest most delicious texture imaginable. When they were on my feet I was transformed to Ariel, Puck and Titania all rolled into one. I danced around the room, feeling as if I were several feet off the ground, turning around and around with the giddy freedom only a winged creature would have. When those enchanting slippers were on my feet, the giggles seemed to come through the soles and shimmy up through my body. These were special shoes, purchased for special occasions and I was not allowed to wear them to play outside the house. However, I thought, what more special occasion was there than my first movie.

I was overjoyed when my father took me in his enormous truck to see my first film, an afternoon matinee of *Bambi* . I wanted to make it more special by wearing my heavenly fairy shoes. What a glorious day was ahead of me - my new shoes, my first movie and a special outing with my father. I climbed into the cab of his truck, being very careful not to put a scratch on them or get them dirty, tucking my feet carefully under me as the truck roared down the country road to nirvana. I was awed by the size of the cavernous dark theater as we entered, for I had never seen anything quite like it. There were rows of seats everywhere and large paintings on the walls. As the movie started, I grabbed my father's hand and stared in awe at the huge figures dominating the screen. I loved Thumper, Flower and, of course, Bambi. When his mother died, the loss he felt was overwhelming. My heart pounded in empathetic anguish over the fear that he must have felt. Bambi's emptiness and confusion washed over me and I couldn't hold back the tears. I sobbed uncontrollable. His loss had become mine. Nothing my father could do would console me and I rode home hiccupping through my tears.

When we reached the house, I eagerly ran in to tell my mother what we had experienced, anticipating her shared joy over my wonderful afternoon. I was shocked to find her at the door twitching with anger. Her eyes flickered down to my feet, and without a word she picked me up and hurled me across the room, slamming me into the wall. I blinked in astonishment. She began screaming, "How could you have worn your new shoes to the movie when you know you weren't allowed to go out of the house with them!" She strode over to me and began hitting me over and over again with a large wooden spoon.

She reached down and ripped the shoes off my feet, yelling, "I'm throwing these in the trash. You can't take care of them, so you can't wear them any more." I wept and begged while she continued to beat me on my head, and arms as I raised them to ward off her blows. My father tried to pull her off me but she was having none of it. I was sent to bed with no supper. I lay in the dark and tried to think what I had done wrong. Somehow I had disobeyed her by wearing my beautiful fairy shoes.

There must have been some compromise reached during the evening, for those shoes were back on the shelf the next day. As I stared at them, unbelieving (for they hadn't been put in the fire or the garbage), I perceived something was different. Instead of my beloved shoes, I saw two black accusing monstrosities reproaching me for disobeying my mother. The magic was gone. I could no longer put them on no matter how much I was coaxed. They reminded me of pain and confusion, and I never again wore my fairy shoes with giggles in the soles.

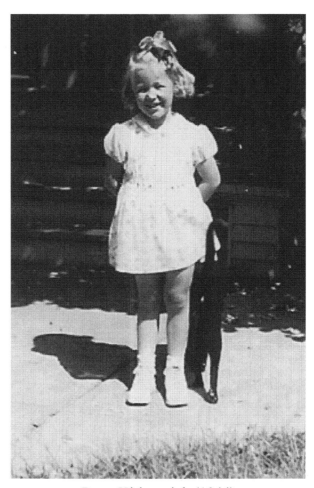

Betty Kirkpatrick (1944)

Bell Bottom Trousers
1944

(Don)

In the summer of 1944 after the smashing success of the Healdsburg Talent Show, the Knights of Pythias decided to have a talent show of their own and they asked members to come up with acts. My mother, a Pythian Sister, entered Betty in the show and the additional rehearsals commenced. Betty was more than willing to practice. On the night of the performance a wide variety of talent performed. Roy Kirkpatrick and Don Frediani played the piano, the Jackson twins sang a duet, Douglas Penry did some magic tricks and Elsie Bonanni sang a solo which filled the hall with magnificent sound. Then Betty, who was four years old, stepped out on the floor. She was the hit of the night as she danced and sang *Bell Bottom Trousers*, with Elmer Sanborn accompanying her. With teary eyes, the audience applauded and cheered until hands were red. The direction of Betty's future was determined.

(Betty)

When I was four, I loved to sing and dance, often dressing in my nightgown because it flowed around my body. I danced for the sheer joy of movement, sometimes pirouetting around the room for no one in particular, but feeling grand and beautiful. If anyone watched, that was good too. One day when we had company, mother said, "Put on your nightgown and show Mrs. Nelson how you dance". Delighted, I eagerly threw it over my head and was transformed into a beautiful ballerina as I began to turn and leap around the room. However, my mother cut me short after only one short turn. "Now you can go to bed. You have your nightgown on."

Despite my protests and tears, I was sent to bed. The nightgown didn't hold magic after that. I saw through my mother that evening and realized she was laughing at the silliness of my dancing in this glorious nightgown and wanted me to dress for bed, not to dance for our company. I never danced for her again.

Bob and Don were great jokers. One day there was a notice for a citywide talent show to be held in Healdsburg. Bob came home, delighted at the great joke he played. "I enrolled Betty in the talent show." he exclaimed, fully expecting his joke to be on the producers of the talent show. After all, how could a four-year old compete. Mother's eyes blazed, "Well, we'll see about this joke." She began to coach me in a song that I loved to sing, *Bell Bottom Trousers,* making me sing it every day until I sang all the words and did a dance to go with it.

On the night of the show, I wore a navy blue sailor dress with a white collar and shoes and stockings to match. As I peeked at the crowd from backstage of the American Legion auditorium I was terrified. The space was enormous and there was sea of faces. I had never seen that many people in one space before and had no idea what to expect. I felt tiny and alone on that huge expanse of stage. The walk from behind the curtains took more courage than I thought I had. What if I failed? What if I fell down? My knees felt as though they wouldn't hold me up. Suddenly the music started and washed over me. My fingers and toes tapped to the rhythm and my insides started to dance. I forgot my fear and all that existed was the music. How I loved singing: *Bell bottom trousers, coat of navy blue. I love a sailor and he loves me too.*

I had never heard applause before, but the sound covered me in a wave of delight. They liked me. My life seemed to be defined in that one moment. I could do something people enjoyed. Here on the stage I was safe. My mother couldn't touch me with her rage.

Elizabeth Dress-up Day

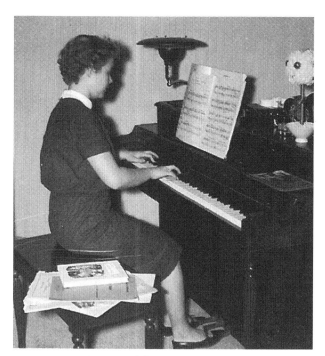

Betty Kirkpatrick (1955)

Piano Lessons 1945-1980

Piano Lessons
1945-1980

(Betty)

Shortly after my singing debut, Mom decided I should begin piano lessons. At about five, I began my weekly visits to Mrs. Hague, an elderly lady who lived on Main Street. Each week I would play little songs like *Airy Fairies and Indian Tom Toms,* but *Shoogy shoe* was my favorite because it had words. I played and sang it for anyone who listened but I was a reluctant pianist. Mother stood over me with a ruler and threatened if I didn't practice. However, I loved to sing.

One particular day I arrived at my piano lesson without eating. I was ravenous. On Mrs. Hague's table was a big bowl of large yellow bananas. As I sat there waiting for my lesson, all I could see was that bowl of gorgeous fruit, and all I could think of was tasting the aromatic sweetness. "Would you like a banana?" she asked as the other student left.

Remembering that my mother said, "Be polite and don't ask for anything", I answered, "It doesn't matter".

"Well", she snapped, "If it doesn't matter, then I suppose you don't want one. Let us begin our lesson." I took that lesson, but for an hour, all I could think about was bananas. When I finished my lesson that day, my teacher saw that I was unhappy. Focusing her gaze on me she said, "You wanted a banana, didn't you?"

I nodded shyly. "Then you must ask for what you want. No one can read your mind. If you want something, you must tell us."

A few days later we had a visitor at the West Grant house, a friend of mother's who wanted to visit with her and see me. She had come before and always handed me a penny as a gift. That day she handed me a penny as before. Having learned my lesson several days before, I stared down at the shiny coin in my hand, looked up at her face and said, "May I have a nickel instead?"

*

I stayed with my lessons, moving from teacher to teacher - a nun at the Catholic School, a woman near the Jr. High School who left piano teaching to go to Hollywood, and finally, to the woman who influenced my life and love of music - Alla Dakserhof. Under Mrs. Dakserhof I left the fluffy repertoire to visit the more serious Bach inventions, Rachmaninoff, Scriabin, Haydn, Beethoven and Chopin. I loved and enjoyed the rigorous Hannon exercises as well as the challenge of great composers. When I was a senior in High School, she informed me I needed to practice one hour a day if I wanted to pass the senior proficiency in the Piano guild. The repertoire was enormous and I needed to play all scales and arpeggios, major and minor.

"But I don't have an hour a day" I complained.
"What is your schedule?" she inquired patiently.

"I get up at 6:30, leave the house at 7:30, finish school at 3:00 and after school I have choir practice, pom pom practice, direct the children's choir at the church etc. etc. I filled in every hour of the day triumphantly.

"I see some time when you can practice." she said quietly.

"Where?" I exclaimed, throwing up my arms.

"From 5:30 to 6:30 in the morning." I gulped, realizing she had found the solution. I was caught. For that year, every morning at 5:30 Pop would wake me and sleepily I sat at the piano and tried to play with the cold light of dawn peeking through the living room window. I learned to play scales while asleep but it only worked for the easy ones with few sharps and flats. I didn't realize at the time the sacrifice my mother and father made, for the piano was on the other side of the wall where my mother slept.

I loved going to Mrs. Dakserhof's house for lessons, and walked the several blocks after church. She fixed something for me to eat, and we progressed to the lesson. She talked about the composer's lives, tested my ear for perfect pitch, talked about opera and opera singers, and provided an open ear for my problems, above all, she taught me to play the piano. One day when I left Mrs. Dakserhof's house, I got into the car, and noticed the anger rising in my mother.

"What do you do in there so long? I don't want you eating there or doing anything other than playing your music. I expect you out in one hour. I will be here waiting, young lady." Thus, my Sunday afternoon sessions were cut short, as was my lifeline to someone who listened to me lovingly, and advised my "IT" life

My friendship with Mrs. Dakserhof stayed with me until she died. She came to my performances at the University of the Pacific, making the arduous four-hour drive to get there. After my opera performance in Verdi's *Masked Ball* she took me aside and said, "You have IT! That is a special quality. That is what will take you far. Remember Dahlink You have "IT". I never forgot those words to me.

Mrs. Dakserhof was an immigrant from Russia, who spoke with a heavy accent. She was deeply ingrained in the classics and knew all aspects of music. She was an opera singer in Russia, and had studied and sung several operatic roles and recitals in her native country. I always wanted to learn to sing and I begged her over and over to teach me to sing, but she refused, saying I should learn the piano better. I accompanied her once on the song *Trees* and was so entranced that I could hardly play the piano.

She took her piano class to the opera in San Francisco several times, introducing us to *Rigoletto,* and *Traviata.* The stories and music entranced me, but I struggled to find the enthusiasm she felt for opera. It wasn't until many years later that I found the passion she conveyed to me long ago in her basement.

North Street

1945 -1949

The Family Portrait
1945

(Betty)

Click: the pain in my head as the fine-toothed comb jerked cruelly through my hair forcing it into submission.

Click: the stiff bristled brush transformed into a weapon when I wiggled.

Click: the triumphal pigtail, tied off with striped ribbons.

Click: the secret hard pinches and hidden head thumps that vented a red-eyed anger.

Click: a reluctant, mute solemn procession, mother striding pulling me by the hand as I stumbled on the cracked sidewalk.

Click: Father carefully placing his feet one after the other as he walked away from the car, his face shuttered against the pain and anguish

Click: Bob and Don trailing behind, quiet, solemn, not saying a word for fear of retribution over a stray hair or a piece of clothing out of place.

Click: The family's feet stumbling over the black rubber treading of the stairs as we climbed to the Photographer's studio.

Click: the steep dark stairway of the building smelling of mildew.

Click: fighting back the tears, which unbidden, rolled down my cheeks.

Click: the abrupt jarring of my teeth as Mother pulled me down hard on the narrow bench beside her.

Click: the fear in my stomach as she thumped her thumb against my head and hissed, "Smile"

Click: the black eye of the camera recording this moment.

Click: There! For all the world to see, within the fragile eggshell of our family, the moment of collective anguish.

Our Mom

Grant School Class (Elizabeth is at the left end of second row.)

Grant School
1945
(Betty)

An old red clopped building sat behind the dilapidated shed, barely big enough to hold our 1937 Chevy. The back seat was my haven, a place to hide and escape. High weeds around the building bordered the graveled yard and rusty frames supported cars and the swing. We loved to be pushed in the swing, going as high as we dared before the jerk and buckle of the wooden seat threw us off. I stood on the seat pumping as high as I dared, sometimes with another child on the seat.

We played in the high grass bordering the schoolyard   we called to each other across the grass rooms-the sweetness of the anise in my head and the cicadas bugs in my ears. When I dared look at the movement of the clouds, I felt the earth move. I would fall off, if I didn't hold tight. -There's a teapot. - There's an elephant.

When I wasn't sitting in the first row of seats in the one room schoolhouse, my favorite pastime was picking wild flowers, which grew, in the prune orchards behind the school. The ground, often full of huge dirt clods plowed in the spring- now covered with new grass and weeds - blue, yellow, white - all were picked to make bouquets. The best flowers were next to the railroad tracks - growing courageously between the wooden railroad ties. These were profuse because they hadn't been subdued by the plow.

Springtime was the best time. The canopy of plum blossoms thick and white overhead - filled the air with intoxicating sweetness because it was a fairy land. The sun transformed the translucent

55

whiteness into a dazzling brilliance, which made my heart turn over with joy. I danced through the trees, a ballerina or crowned princess, my imagined roles billowed into the air around me.

My afternoon nap was the time I took solitary sojourns into the magic playground behind the school where my mother couldn't see me. I spent most days in the cavernous back seat of our family car - my cheek often itchy from the rough brown seat cover where I laid my head to sleep.

*

The schoolhouse seemed enormous, eight rows of seats, rigidly marking the territory of each grade. Some of the rows were full to the back, and some had only two children. Each day began with the Pledge of Allegiance and a chorus of *My Country 'tis of Thee*. Voices raised in various styles of tunefulness, all ages to be finished with the ritual, some hushing, some raising heads to roar out the high note. I loved this tune and eagerly looked forward to singing with everyone as a five year old - it was my moment to be one of the big kids.

The day commenced with assignments given to each grade. Each child waited the allotted time when they met with the teacher, my mother. The first grade, where I sat, was given reading and writing work to do. I was sent outside to hear the alphabet of the other four first graders and to be certain it was correct. I would sit in the back of the room and listen to them read from the primer; correcting the faulty pronunciation and helping slower students recognize the more difficult words. The days we had art projects were special because we got to work with the older kids. Sometimes the entire school worked on the same project, digging up clay under the tree at the side of the building and mixing it with water to maker pots, plates and vases.

After lunch students gathered quietly while mother read chapters from books - the classics- such as Black Beauty and King Arthur. I sat in a small chair in the front row and listened intently, loving the stories and adventures.

*

One day when we were ready to leave school, the old Chevy wouldn't start. Repeated chugging wouldn't budge it. Mother sent one of the older students into town for a tow truck, and after an interminable time they returned. The tow-truck cranked up the car and hauled it into town. I watched Mother becoming more and more anxious, turning into the demon, she sometimes was. That evening she burst into the house with murder in her eyes, "Rocks in my gas tank. Someone put rocks in my gas tank." I scuttled into the corner to avoid the white-hot anger. Seeing me in the corner she ran over and began to beat me, first with her hand, and as the minutes went by with whatever she could find, "You did it - admit it."

I gulped down my fear and stammered, "N-N-No-I didn't, I d-d-don't know what you are talking about." Yanking me up by my arm, she shoved me down the back steps and strode over to the prune tree in the back yard. Pulling off a sturdy branch, she began to switch me on my legs, arms, back, and neck, screaming at me, I maintained my innocence and was sent to bed with no supper. I slept fitfully for I feared she would yank me out of bed and begin the beating again.

The fury had not abated the next morning and again I was beaten before we left for school. "Admit it. Admit it." But I held fast saying I had not done it. "Admit it and I will stop beating you.," she screeched.

As tempting as that was, I maintained my innocence saying, "How can I say I did it, when I didn't?" That day she was so furious that she wouldn't allow me into the school, I had to stay locked in the car in the old shed. She came out every half hour to make sure I was still there. At lunchtime she gave me my lunch. I was grateful to be away from her anger for the day but very lonely, as no one was allowed to talk to me.

That evening I expected to see her anger abated but it was still there. She strode to the car as red-hot as ever. I was deathly frightened for I couldn't imagine another evening with the switch. "You did it, you little liar," she yelled. "I stood all the boys in a row and asked who did it, and they said they didn't, so it had to be you." I knew the boys were afraid, for Mother had the habit of punishing students by hitting their hands with a ruler, breaking it sometimes. I recall her turning a young man over her knee and spanking him with a ruler, his bare buttocks seen by everyone.

I couldn't understand why she believed the fourth and fifth grade boys but not me. That night the switch came out again and in fear and pain I screamed that I did it for she said she would stop beating me if I said so. In a rage she took the yardstick and began beating me. My arms were already black and blue and red welts were still hurting on my legs as I screamed.

The beating didn't stop but now she told me it was because I had lied. I learned that day that it doesn't matter if you are guilty or innocent, you will still be punished. I had lied, when I told her "I did it," She never discovered who put rocks in the gas tank.

*

One early morning the kids were playing in front of the school waiting for it to begin. Albert, an eighth grader, was assigned to ring the school bell announcing the start of school. We swung on the bars and rungs and one the boys lifted me up so I could swing, too. He held me as I gripped the rings high above the ground. Albert had lowered the chain on one of the rings so I could grab it more easily. They began swinging the ring back and forth and on one return, it hit me just above the eye. We all ran up the steps when we heard the school bell ring. Mother stood in the doorway making note of who was late or absent that day. When she saw me she started to scream. Puzzled, I put my hand to my eye, which felt funny. It came back bloody. I started to screech and cry as well. Mother told Albert to put me in the car. She ran into the school and told Gloria Petroncelli to take charge while she was gone. Gloria agreed and we left for the hospital. By then I had stopped crying because I was secretly in love with Albert and he was in the back seat with me. The doctor stitched me up and I was taken home for a bowl of soup and some comfort. Eventually Albert had to go back to school and leave me. When mother returned to school she expected chaos, because she had left the children unattended for three hours. But as she entered the room, instead of noise, everyone was sitting quietly at his or her desk doing the assigned work. A disaster was averted.

On the Bus to Fort Bragg
1945

(Betty)

Our family was well acquainted with the Finnish side of the family as most of mother's relatives lived in Fort Bragg, a small logging town on the northern California coast. To go there was an adventure, for it required traveling in our old Chevy over the two-lane highway winding through brown hills on the way to the coast. What we consider picturesque now, was to be endured in those days. I stared out the back window of the car three hours at the slow procession of ancient fence posts, moss covered threes, and crusty dry hills dotted with scrubby oak. It was an adventure to stop in Boonville and have pie at the *Horn of Zeese* or pause in the shadows of the huge redwoods while the Finnish *Laipa* came out and the thermos of coffee appeared. I was offered lemon drops, which I greedily sucked hoping for more. When we climbed the last hill and caught the breathtaking view of the ocean, I knew my arduous trip was almost over. Bouncing around in the cavernous back seat of the Chevy, I was usually car sick – the nausea quickly subsided as I descended eagerly in front of 304 Morrow Street to greet the smile of aunt Ino.

When I was five, mother dressed me in my red coat and hat and gave me a little suitcase to go "solo" to Fort Bragg on the bus. It was my annual trip to stay with aunts Ino and Mayme for a week. I looked forward to the responsibility of traveling on my own and being with my sunny aunts and uncles – away from the unpredictable temper of mother, for she never traveled without several angry outbursts. I had a peanut butter and jelly sandwich wrapped in wax paper and an apple carefully snuggled in the small brown paper bag I carried firmly in one hand. Nina my rag doll and constant companion, was clutched tightly in the other.

"Don't talk to strangers" Mother admonished.

"Yes Momma"

"Stay on the Bus and only get off if you have to"

"Yes Momma"

"Don't sit on the toilet seat"

"Yes Mama" I replied, climbing up the steep steps of the bus. I walked towards the back and found seat two thirds of the way back. I waved goodbye and anticipated a wonderful week.   As the bus began to snake the twisty trail over the mountains, I slid back and forth on the hard leather bench seat. I tried grabbing the bar on the seat in front of me but it didn't help. Back and forth I went as the bus rounded each curve. I felt the familiar nausea rising, only this time it was aggravated by the passengers all smoking around me. As the trip progressed, the air became thick and blue with smoke. By the time we arrived in Boonville I was anxious to get off the bus and get away from the smoke but I could hardly walk and mother's words were ringing in my ears. "What would happen if I got off and the bus pulled away?

"Would you like to come with me to the ladies room?" The sweet-faced lady smiled and coaxed me off the bus. The rest room was littered with toilet paper on the floor and the wastebasket was filled to the brim, obviously it had not been cleaned for a long time. The toilet seat was so high I couldn't get up without help and Mother had told me not to sit on the toilet seat.   I decided that the best way to go was in the corner. Just as I was about to go, the lady came in the rest room and saw what I was starting to do.

"Oh no, Dear, don't do that – you must use the toilet."

"But my mother said I shouldn't sit on the seat and I can't get up there."

She gingerly lifted me and showed me how to sit on my hands while I went to the bathroom. On the way back to the bus, she bought me a bottle of Nehi, which was delicious.

It was such a relief to see my Aunt Ino and Uncle Bob waiting for me as the bus turned the corner in Fort Bragg. They had big smiles and lots of waves. The cool damp air was such a relief from the smoky interior of the bus that my difficult adventure was quickly forgotten. I found my sea legs again traversing the small patch of grass that grew outside the front of their house.

Manda and John Aikaa
1945

(Betty)

We moved to North Street when I was five. " Imagine," I thought, "moving to town and we would no longer live in the country with cows and chickens." The house Pop built on North Street was just blocks away from the town center. It was set back a distance from the street with a few straggly prune trees in the front yard. I was in heaven. Here I had people to play with. Gail Grove, who lived with her grandmother across the street, Stevie Meade and Bobby Fistolara who lived down the block were all my playmates. Halloween was fun, for I could dress up as I pleased and traipse up and down the block trick or treating.

One year there was a parade and a prize was given for the best costume. I dressed up in my favorite role as a queen with the neighborhood children as attendants. How grand it was to walk down the street in the gold colored silk dress with mountains of skirt, a gift from a family friend. I had a crown and scepter. When the time came to declare the winner, we all crowded together, holding our collective breath. We won. The grand prize was $2.00. How proudly I carried the money, for I never saw that much money at one time before. When I got home, mother took the two one-dollar bills from me and handed me four fifty-cent pieces. "You have to give the money to the neighborhood children who were with you." I was six, but I knew that four attendants at fifty cents apiece equaled two dollars. "But that's all the money." I exclaimed "and it was my idea and I won."

"They were a part of it and they won too, so the money needs to be divided."

"But I won't get anything."

"You get the glory," my mother answered.

I went to their houses and gave each of my friends fifty cents, but I never understood why the money couldn't have been divided five ways.

*

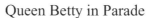

Queen Betty in Parade

When I was seven, my mother's cousins Manda and John Aikaa came from Redding to live with us. They were delightful - especially Manda, and I adopted her immediately as my grandmother. For the few short months she was with us, she managed to help settle the family boat and things were on an even keel. They stayed in my brothers' room over the garage while John built a house on the lot next to us. Manda cooked the meals, which were unusual and wonderful. She had been a cook with major corporative families in the Bay Area, and she was a fantastic cook. I had my first taste of brains and tripe, and rejected them both. I loved her tongue because we could eat the fuzzy end. I found it wonderful and gross at the same time. In those years we came as close to a normal family life as I remember. For years afterwards I enjoyed visiting Manda and John, and we played Pinochle. John was a terrific player, but a poor sport. He didn't like losing. Manda and John didn't have much money, and one night, I discovered them sitting in the dark to save money

Manda gave wonderful dinner parties and always had *laipa* made for anyone who happened to be visiting them. One never entered a Finnish household without being served *laipa* and coffee. We sat around the table while everyone conversed in Finnish. My father, my brothers and I would eat *laipa,* drink coffee or lemonade, listen but not understand. I thought it strange mother didn't teach us Finnish, but I realized later, it was her way of maintaining distance or keeping secrets. I learned certain words and I knew if they were talking about me - *piccu tutu* - Little girl, *kaku tutu* - bad girl, *hueva tutu* - good girl. When she gave parties, the table groaned with food. Large salad platters were arranged like works of art with carved vegetables and flowers with a ring of tomato aspic in the center. Butter was always in fancy shapes like crisscrossed balls or lilies with long stamens. I once tied forming the lilies with the two paddles she used, but only made a mess.

Her house seemed to be a mecca for the large Finnish family on my mother's side. They always gathered there when they came to town.

Onnie Lattu, Shirley, Newt, Manda Aikaa

The Grammar School
1933-1945

(Bob)

In 1933 I went to kindergarten in an old building on Tucker Street behind the Catholic Church. The new Grammar School was under construction and school classes were being housed all over town. My first grade class was in a building behind the American Legion building further up the street. There were three cannons in front of the Legion building and we felt well guarded. In 1934 my second grade teacher was Mrs. Fields and our class was part of the first group of students to go to school in the new Grammar School. We felt it was a great honor. I spent my next seven years in that building.

(Don)

In 1936 I attended kindergarten in the new Grammar School. There were several teachers in my class that year but they made little impression on me and I do not remember their names. My first grade teacher was Mrs. Schwab, who was an "old school" teacher. She was disciplined, severe and tolerated no nonsense in her classroom. She taught the Palmer method of penmanship and required her students to write with circles and slanted lines.

Healdsburg Grammar School First Grade 1937

I had Mrs. Fields in the second grade and Mrs. Young in the third. Mrs. York had grades three and four and although my mother didn't want me in a combination classroom, the alternative, Mrs. Meisner, was mean and not acceptable to Mom or me.

My fifth grade teacher was Mrs. Combs and two things stand out in my memory. Rollie Robinson did not pay attention and his jabber continually interrupted the class. When Mrs. Combs could not stand it any longer, she broke a yardstick on his back and a piece flew across the room. At recess, the conversation was not about Rollie being struck, but about how big the broken piece was. I won the argument when I pulled the piece out of my pocket. "It was three and a half inches."

Legible writing was important to Mrs. Combs and one day she selected two students with bad handwriting and made arrangements with Mrs. Schwab to have them report to the first grade classroom for an hour a day for two weeks to learn how to write. The two were David Gilbert and I. I was so embarrassed that I vowed to myself, I would **never** write legibly. I have kept that vow for many years.

Richard Rowe was a well-developed eighth grade playground bully. He and his family were migrant workers from Oklahoma. Folks in the community called them "Oakies" often in a derogatory way. Richard dominated the playground culture with his fists and his loud voice. He worked his way through the eighth and seventh grades and everyone was afraid of him. I was a fairly well developed sixth grader and was one of his targets. One day he approached me on the playground and gave me a shove. For the first time in my life I lost my temper and took out after him. When I tackled him, sat on his chest and pummeled him, he offered little resistance. The yard duty teacher pulled us apart and marched us in to see Mr. Gibbs, the principal. He lectured us in a stern voice about fighting on the playground and we were sentenced to time in the detention room after school. I glanced at Mr. Gibbs as we left the office and saw him cover a smile with his hand. Richard eased off his bullying behavior and for some time afterward, I was a playground hero. That day I learned two things; a bully can also be a coward and when you stand on an issue, do it with firmness.

Miss Shanahan was my sixth grade teacher and she was tough but fair. She insisted that writing and math assignments be neat and correct. If errors were found, the entire paper had to be recopied. And turned in again. When the year finally ended we breathed a collective sigh of relief. Then we discovered that the seventh and eighth grades were to be departmentalized with Mrs. Luce teaching English, Mr. Manley, math, and Miss Shanahan social studies. We were not free from her after all.

My eighth grade year was a busy one. I played in the band, competed on the track squad and the basketball team. I ran for student body president against Keith Walker and won. As student body president, I was the master of ceremonies at our eighth grade graduation. It was there I learned to use notes. I had memorized several paragraphs, which were to precede each of four student speakers. Unfortunately, I gave the introductory paragraphs in the wrong order and the students' topics did not match their talks. The students gave their talks as scheduled. I expected a reprimand from Mr. Manley but he congratulated me and said "No-one knew the difference."

The Campaign: Kirk for President
Aldo Belagio, Art Gully, Emil Passalacqua, George Izzet, Bill McDonald, David Gilbert.
D Kirkpatrick, Bill Stine, Ben Cimoli, Mit Runnells, Ernie Frandsen

Our elementary school basketball team had a successful season, winning seven and losing two. In the opening game we defeated a team from Litton Home. The Tribune said they were "drubbed by a score of 30 to 10." The team continued to win games and their activities were faithfully reported by Chris Jennings who always seemed to get his nephew, Jimmy Jennings, named in the paper. At the end of the season, we were awarded block "H"s. Mom sewed mine on a sweater and I wore it with pride. Morris Ruby was the coach and shortly after the season was over, he took me aside and suggested that I spend less time on the basketball court and more time practicing the hundred-yard dash. I did and later ran dashes for the high school track team. The last time I checked, a plaque on the wall of the gym, indicated I held the record for the 120-yard dash. It helps to know that race was discontinued a couple years after my record was set. Four years later in a rematch for H.S. Student Body President, I suffered the first defeat of my political career. Keith Walker, who had grown into a tall handsome basketball star won easily as the election was held shortly after the basketball season was over. That year I tried out for the Dramatics Club.

The Elementary Basketball Team
1945
Back: Morris Ruby (coach), Eugene Cade, David Manley, Keith Walker, Jim Jennings, D Kirkpatrick, Art Gully,

Front: Stan Smith, Ernie Frandsen, Alfred Elgin, Richard Jacobsen, Ted Gibbs, manager)

The 8th Grade graduating class of 1945

Irene Long, English Teacher @ Healdsburg High

The Hamlet Quest
1947

(Don)

Little did Miss Long know when she hammered her English students over the head with Shakespeare, her influence would trigger an unintended event. It was the summer of 1947, and I had just finished my sophomore year in high school. When someone discovered Lawrence Olivier was to play Hamlet at the Curren Theater, it was our chance to see a master of the stage in person.

The Pierce boys managed to secure their family Studebaker for the trip. All of the gang wanted to go but only one vehicle was available. The car held six, but we squeezed in seven. Shirley would have made eight and to her lifelong chagrin, she remained at home. Dick was the driver and Alberta was his date. Hap, Roger, and I squeezed into the back seat with Margy sitting on my lap.

Lawrence Olivier made Hamlet come alive that night and our emotions rode high when we left the theater. We approached the Bridge on the way home and Rob and Hap, who had no female distraction, discussed in detail the various features of the Golden Gate Bridge.
Rob said, "Hap, look at that tower. I heard it is about 750 feet to the water from up there. Imagine the view from the top......You know, it wouldn't be all that hard to climb up the cable."

Hap replied with more than casual interest because he loved to climb. "Well .... I guess it would be quite a sight."

After we passed the tollgate, Dick, decided to call their bluff. And pulled over to the edge of the road, "OK it's all yours."

Rob leaped out, "Come on, Hap. Dick, meet us on the other side of the bridge." Hap extracted himself from the back seat and the two of them disappeared into the low-hanging fog shrouding the Golden Gate Bridge.

Dick muttered, "They're just going to walk across the bridge." We drove to the other side where we parked the car and waited. Dick and Alberta conversed quietly in the front seat, and I flirted with Margy in the back. Roger was asleep in his corner. About an hour and a half elapsed and we began to get uneasy. Roger woke up and in an almost inaudible voice whispered "It shouldn't take that long to walk over the bridge."

The deep resonance of a motorcycle splintered the silence. A leather booted patrolman, sauntered over to the car and stomped his foot on the running board. Cigarette dangling from his mouth, he growled, "What are you kids doing here? Can't you find a better place to park?"

Dick replied tentatively "Officer, we're just waiting for two of our friends who are walking

67

across the bridge."

The patrolman replied gruffly "I just came over the bridge and there are **no** walkers on it. We discourage pedestrians at night."

That statement frightened us and Roger whimpered from the back seat: "They said something about climbing to the top of the tower."

The officer's foot dropped to the ground, and his cigarette fell from his mouth. "Oh my God. .... You kids wait **right** here until I come back. Don't move." And he roared off.

About ten minutes later an exhausted Rob and Hap appeared through the mist and dragged themselves into the car. We did not wait for the patrolman to return. Dick simply stepped on the starter, gunned the motor and said, "Let's get outta here**.**"

"Where have you guys been? Didn't the cop see you on the bridge? What took you so long?" Roger looked at his older brother, "Did you *really* climb all the way to the top? "

Rob held up his red and blistered hands and let out a sigh. "You... should... have... seen the view. "

The Song of the Flea
1947

(Betty)

When we were at North Street, Pop built a room above the garage for my two brothers. It seemed like a paradise to me, and when they were away at school, I crept up the stairs and sat on the colorful striped wool blanket reading some of my favorite Big Little books. These wonderful precursors to our modern day comics lined the walls of my brothers' room. I was careful with them as it was stated clearly to me I wasn't to touch them. I took them down, devoured them and then placed them exactly as I found them. I adored listening to a 78 record of Chaliapin singing Musorgsky's "song of the Flea". I closed my eyes and let the "Ha ha ha ha ha, the flea, ha ha ha ha ha, the flea" shiver up my spine. I sang that phrase reliving the pure delight the voice and song gave me. I played the record over and over, until the story the singer told in that mellifluous voice was memorized. Whenever I was punished or sad, this room was my haven and the record never failed to cheer me up.

One day after a particularly difficult beating, I crept up the stairs sobbing, looking forward to the music. I knew as soon as I heard the "ha ha ha ha ha the flea" I would smile inside and begin to heal. When I took the record out of the case, I gasped with shock – it was broken. What a blow she had discovered my hideaway. I would never hear that wonderful sound again. I felt the magical balm was gone forever. Later that day Mother told me sternly I couldn't go upstairs any more and she had broken the record when she was cleaning. It wasn't until 60 years later that I surmised the truth – it wasn't an accident. She did the same to my brother's "Big Rock Candy Mountain."

A Big Little Book

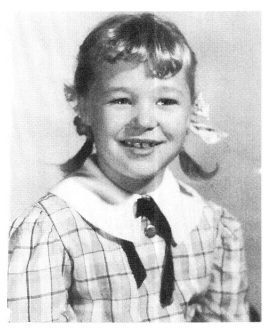

Betty Kirkpatrick

Washing in the Tub
1948

(Betty)

Mama always washed the clothes in a divided cement tub with a wringer mounted between the two sinks. The clothes were scrubbed on one side, and then carefully fed through the wringer to come out the other, compressed and shapeless, not resembling our familiar shirts, skirts, pants and nightgowns. We shook them out and hung them to dry on the line. She was rarely in a good mood when performing this task, slapping the clothes hard against the tub before their journey through the wringer. Watching her pendulous breasts hanging loosely in her wash dress reminded me of her mother who lost a breast - caught in the wringer. When I was particularly dirty, after a rousing day of crawling on my stomach under the house, climbing a tree or playing cowboys and Indians, she stripped me for a bath in one of the tubs. When she was angry, she shoved me around and occasionally banged my head on the cement tub. I never did get my hand put through the wringer as she so often threatened.

One day she seemed more angry than usual as she washed me in the tub, and banged my bony elbows and legs against the sides. I was starting to grow, my arms and legs extended over the tub like a grasshopper. At eight years of age, I felt self conscious and awkward, being bathed in the tub this way.

"You are sickly white" she exclaimed. "You need sun." She opened the back door and pushed me outside, naked in the early spring morning.

"Please - let me back in the house" I shivered through my tears, trying to cover my nakedness with my hands.

"No, you stay out there until you get some color".

I was afraid someone would see me so I huddled into a ball on the lawn, but the stiff brown grass felt like sharp needles on my skin. I crawled under a bush in the back yard and sat there for several hours, frightened and cold. I heard a car pull up and the door slam shut. The approaching footsteps came closer and closer. They echoed up the back steps and I crawled further back into the bushes for fear of being seen. It was the plumber who came to unplug a sink. He worked on the plumbing and finally left. I was convinced that my mother would come outside to get me while he was there, and pull me naked into the house in front of him.

When mother unlocked the door later, she ridiculed me exclaiming "Why are you afraid of being naked? It doesn't matter, you are just a young girl." I was relieved to be let back into the house and was still crying when I ran up the back stairs and tried to get past my mother. I didn't quite make it, for she slapped me hard on my backside as I ran by. She often called these slaps "love pats" but they stung long after, and I felt the sharp anger contained in them.

Elizabeth Kirkpatrick Second Grade circa 1948

The Junior Statesmen Summer School @ Montezuma 1948

Don & Clinky
1948

(Don)

In High School I was active in the Dramatics Club, and I participated on the varsity track and football teams. In my junior year, I ran for Student Body President but was defeated. In the summer of 1948, I was awarded a scholarship with the Junior Statesman Organization. This was an eight week Summer Session at the Montezuma School for Boys in Los Gatos. I was seventeen and at least ten letters were exchanged between my seven-year-old sister and me during the time I was there. Betty, who I called Clinky, wrote, addressed, and mailed the letters by herself. The spelling and punctuation is presented as it was in the letters.

In the picture above the third person from the left in the back row is Edwin Meese III who served as Attorney General from 1985-1988 under President Ronald Reagan. I am the third person from the right in the front row.

July 4, 1948
Dear Don Hi!
How are you? I am fine. I past my swimming test. We (the family) are going Down to the beach today. Jee I'm glad today is the 4 of July. Daddy lost his knife again and that little girl found it.
Betty xxxxxx oooooo

9, 1948
Dear Don
How are you? I am fine. I am getting along nicely in my swimming lessons. My garden is awful. But Bobby's garden is nice. Thank you four the little donkey. Bobby keeps the lawn mowed. The new lawn is ready Mother can't talk because (other side) her top teeth are out but that is a secret.

She gets them back Saturday, Would you like me to send you some food for bedtime? I am flattening bottle caps then I am to make a hole in the bottle cap then I am going to put them on a tambourine
 good bye
Betty
 xxxxxxxxxxxxx oooooooooooo

July 11, 1948
Dear Betty,

I'm glad to hear that you passed your swimming test, also that you won a prize in swimming contest. Congratulations.
I'm in quite a hurry this morning, because I'm going to church in Los Gatos. So this letter will have to be brief. I find it hard to find time to write many letters they keep us so busy. For instance Friday I worked for almost six hours on homework alone, not counting cleaning our room and etc. As you can see this doesn't give us much time for recreation.
Is "cookie" getting big? She should be quite a cat by now.
Well I must be signing off. Bye Now.
Love,
Don

July 14, 1948
Dear Don

I got a sand Box now. Do you know a Poem Hush be still ? It goes like this. Hush be still as my mouse, There's a Stranger in our house. Not a Dolly, not a toy but a baby-bouncing boy. Mothers making apricot jam. Bobby has a vegetable and fruit market across from buffis hotel
by now
Betty
xxxxxx oooooo

July 14, 1948
Dear Clinky, Hi !

I'm sorry your garden isn't doing so well. Why don't you work on it more ? How are your piano lessons coming along ? How much does Bob make in one day on his Drive in? That is much more than I expected - all that publicity- Maybe some day Bob's name will be in lights.
---- Kirkpatrick's food chain -----
Speaking of food - I think I could use a little bedtime snack once in a while. We eat three times a day and no matter how much I eat, I am still hungry at bedtime. You write a pretty good letter but watch your spelling a bit. You used the wrong kind of for (Four) once. Now I want to write a page to Mom.
So Long
Love
Don xxoxxooxooxxoox

Sunday July 18,1948

Dear Don

How are you? I am fine. You better watch your spelling. for raisins you put R-a-i-s-e-n-s. You better look on the raisin package that moms sending you. Mom made some fudge and cookies too.

My piano lessons are getting along nicely. The Carnival is in town. Pop is putting tile board in the bathroom today. I joined the reading Club. If I read 20 books I get a cowboy. Charlene did not come today.

good by xxxxxxxxx oooooooooo

love

Betty

July 18,1948

Dear Clinky, Hi !

That's a pretty nice poem. Did you write it yourself? Where did Mom get the apricots to make jam with ? In this county there are loads of apricots in the country. In fact there are orchards and orchards full of them, The school has an apricot cannery of their own, later on when they get ripe some of us will work in the cannery, maybe.

I just got back from a tennis game - **Wow** !- is it hot up here. What kind of sand have you in your sand - box ?

Well Bye for now.

Don oxxooxxoox

P.S. Mom, Don't be surprised if 2 other fellows and I come home some weekend. ----Probably not next weekend

July 26, 1948

Dear Don

How are you ? I am fine, do you remember that Snow White Puzzle ? Well its all finished. I have white sand in my sandbox. Bobby gave Mom The apricots to make jam with. Did you forget about Pops birthday Bobby gave him a belt. Mom gave him a pipe. I gave him some underwear.

by xxxxxxxxxxx ooooooooooo

love

Betty

P.S. hi thanks for the Donkey

(Date unreadable)

Dear Don

How are you ? I am fine. Thank you for the key ! When I was at Bobs Store mom gave me some jumping beans, I am sending you one. This is how you work one. take a piece of toilet paper and put the jumping Bean on it then it will jump.

by now

xxxxxxxxxxxxx ooooooooooooo

love

Betty

P.S. thanks again for the key

August 6, 1948
Dear Clinky, Hi !
How are you ? That's good. How did you like Vacation Bible School? I guess two of us have gone to school this summer.
I am sitting in Constitutionalism class now, supposed to be taking notes; but I'm tired of taking notes. Have you been swimming lately? How did you like the fair? I'm sorry that I couldn't be there. Thank you very much for the jumping bean, I will certainly get a lot of enjoyment out of it. How is Bob's store coming along?
Thank you very much again for the jumping bean.
Love
oxooxxo
Don
P.S. You're welcome for the key.

Observations: I think Betty won the duel of the xxs and oos. In Betty's July 9 letter, she believed that our Mom would get her own teeth back. The prize that Betty won in the swimming contest was for coming in last. I was not able to arrange the surprise visit home.

Jr. Statesmen Summer School Graduates (1948)

1st Row: Frank Ephraim, Jack Curtis, Gene Burd, Randall Reid 2nd Row: Charles Shields, Kenneth Johnson, Lee Corbin, Al Gerow, Ben Veit, Max McDonald, Don Price
3rd Row: **Ed Meese**, Jack Teeters, Lee Adams, Jon Chapin 4th Row: **Don Kirkpatrick**, Jim Makshanoff, Jere Barlow, William Shearer, Herbert Ellingwood

Healdsburg High School 1949
An Unwitting Accomplice
1948-49

(Don)

During the school year of 1948-49, my friends and I were enthralled by what we learned in Jim Vogt's Chemistry Class. We studied the periodic table and discovered Hydrogen sulfide smells like rotten eggs. My good friend, Rob Pierce was an excellent student and was so enamored with chemistry, he made his life work in that field. He became a professional chemist and a multimillionaire filling government contracts during the Viet Nam war.

Some of the rest of us saw the knowledge gleaned from Mr. Vogt's class as a means to an end of a short-term objective. When Mr. Vogt demonstrated how to make fuses from potassium nitrate and string, a light bulb went off in my head.

The study hall was on the first floor of the school and when Mr. Fletcher, not the most observant teacher in the world, was in charge, we realized it was possible to climb out a window in the back of the room without being observed. This gave some of the more adventurous among us a chance to explore the nooks and crannies of the building.

Bertha Vranna's Spanish and Algebra classes were on the third floor of the high school building. Bertha did not understand it was her shrill voice and uptight responses to out of the ordinary behavior, which made her a target for practical jokes. In the spring of 1948, someone planted a smoke bomb in Miss

Vranna's car. The word around campus was that David Cootes and Robert Simon did it, but Bud Christensen, the principal. was never able to pin the culprits down.

Previously, David Gilbert and I had discovered a door leading to the attic was not always locked. We escaped from study hall, climbed the ladder, and discovered that by putting our ears to the large metal air vents, which extended from the attic to the classrooms, we could hear what was going on. Because the timbre of her voice was amplified in the air vents, it was easy to recognize Miss Vranna's classroom.

I whispered to Dave, "I have an idea, remember those fire crackers I have left over from last July? I'll bet they would make a pretty loud noise in Miss Vranna's vent. Let's make a long fuse in chem lab and hang the firecrackers in the vent."

Dave responded, "That could be pretty spectacular."

Bertha Vranna, Spanish and Math teacher

We made fuses of varying length and timed how long they would burn. We tied a fuse to the bundle of firecrackers, lit it and carefully lowered it into the vent. We were running around the track in 6th period P.E. when the sound of a loud explosion reverberated from the top floor of the school. I think Bud Christensen suspected who might have been responsible, but he had no proof. Until now no one has owned up to that outrageous prank. I wonder if anyone ever asked Mr. Vogt which students seemed unduly interested in learning how to make fuses.

77

Bud Christensen, Principal

(Don)

Post Script: On November 26, 2011, Jim Vogt celebrated his 100th birthday. He died on May 4, 2012. Over the years both David Gilbert and I completed our education with Ph.D.'s. David spent his career as an English Professor at a University in Washington. I worked forty years in Education, with more than twenty as a school superintendent in several different districts.

Bob's Fruit Market
1949

(Don)

It was the summer of 1949. My brother Bob had finished his two-year stint in the Navy and one year at Santa Rosa Junior College. I graduated from Healdsburg High School and we were looking forward to the next year at U.C. Berkeley. Bob looked at life's potential with big eyes, and came up with an idea to build a fruit stand as our way to make money for the summer. I think our father suggested the idea because he didn't have much work for the two of us. However, the energy and drive to make it happen came from Bob.

Pop owned an empty lot on the highway just south of the railroad tracks, a perfect location for a fruit stand. He was a building contractor and from the time we could walk, Bob and I knew how to pound a nail. When we were adolescents we could build a stud wall and shingle a roof. That summer we pooled our savings of $1500, bought the lumber, and the three of us erected a building to house the Fruit Market. Two weeks later we put up our shingle and were in business.

Neither Bob nor I had worked in a grocery store so we had no idea how to set a price on a potato or a pound of tomatoes. We visited the local markets and wrote down prices they charged. We figured since we had no employees and no overhead, we could sell for less and still make a profit. We did not figure on spoilage---yet.

We had no trouble getting fruit and vegetables. The local farmers came to us and we bought what they offered and paid what they said it was worth. One day a man came by with a huge truckload of watermelons. We weren't sure if watermelons would sell, but the price seemed right, and we bought the entire load. We didn't realize how many melons a truck held and found the gigantic pile occupied a third of our store's space. Our family ate a lot of melons that summer.

The Fruit Market was nine hundred square feet with a shake roof. The front and sides were enclosed with removable screen panels. The bins we built held a lot of potatoes and onions, which didn't seem to spoil. Since we had no refrigeration or coolers, we soon discovered lettuce, eggplants, cucumbers and tomatoes did not do well in the summer heat of Healdsburg. Our conclusion was to move the produce quickly. Bob made a deal with Pop to borrow his truck and take the vegetables to the customers.

Our run was down Matheson Street and around Fitch Mountain. We targeted the beaches along the Russian River where summer visitors hung out. The Fitch Mountain run was successful, but our pricing structure did not take into account the cost of operating the truck. When one of us was on the mountain run, the other had to operate the store by himself. When we used the restroom in the service station across the street, the store had to be closed, which meant the sliding wire screen doors had to be locked. We thought twice about going for a pee break.

July can be warm in Sonoma County and as the days got hotter, the leafy greens wilted and the tomatoes grew mushy. No matter how much we sprinkled and covered them for the night, the next morning they didn't look the same. The faster our vegetables spoiled, the more generous we became. It was apparent we needed to keep our store open longer to accommodate evening shoppers, and we extended store hours to 8:00 in the evening.

Twelve-hour days in the sizzling heat of Healdsburg made the summer of '49 a long one, and we were glad to see it come to a close. When we tallied up receipts and subtracted costs, we made approximately fifty cents an hour. At the end of the summer, we sold the Fruit Market to some Italian folks, who moved it across the highway where it became a much larger place with coolers. It has operated in its new location as a viable business for many years. When we went to U.C. Berkeley that fall, we both decided teaching school might be an easier way to earn a living. We changed our majors from business administration to education.

Don & Bob (1949)

Roy Rogers & Dale Evans

Saturday afternoon at the Movies
1949

(Betty)

Mother was fond of chanting: Monday, washday, Tuesday ironing, Wednesday, canning and on through the week. Eventually she came to Saturday, which was cleaning day. I was not allowed to go anywhere until my contributions to this ritual were finished, so I gathered the trash and burned it outside in a big rusty can. I enjoyed this on a nice day but in the winter when it was cold I would stamp my feet to keep warm and tuck my hands under my armpits to be able to feel my fingers again. Dusting was an onerous chore as I was instructed to lift each object and dust under it. The rag, which had a former life as a shirt or nylon undershirt, was carefully doused with oil before I began. When I wiped the table I buffed it hard with another dry cloth until the oil was gone and the table shone. My particular dislike was the side table filled with small carved ivory birds which had to be placed back exactly as I found them. I loved running the rag over the face of the carved trunk my brother Bob sent from the orient. I traced the walking figures and imagined stories about the dragons or fisherman, which curved up over the top. Next I dust-mopped the floors until they shone. I didn't like dragging the ancient canister vacuum around the living room, for the hose, electric cord and wand never cooperated by remaining connected at the same time. I hung the laundry on the line outside and it was a game to see if I could get all the laundry up before I ran out of clothespins.

When the chores were done I was given a quarter to go the movies about six blocks away. I loved going for it seemed as if the entire grammar school was there. It didn't matter what was playing, we all went just to see each other out of school. I had the five cents necessary for a candy bar but I almost never had the enormous amount of ten cents for popcorn. It wouldn't have mattered anyway, for most of the kids; especially the boys used it for ammunition to get our attention during the advertisements. We endured the newsreels and the singing, dancing flowers in the Felix the Cat cartoon in order to get to the serials, which we followed every week. We wondered what would happen next to Tarzan. My favorite movies were the ones with Roy Rogers. "What a handsome man he was." I swooned with the rest of the girls as we watched him gallop across the screen on Trigger, the most beautiful and intelligent horse on the planet and argue with Gabby Hayes, a rough talking bearded sidekick. I proclaimed to the world that I would marry Roy Rogers when I grew up. He inspired me to a short-lived passion for a horse.

When I was nine there was a contest with "a weeks' stay at his ranch" offered as the prize. I entered and eagerly waited for the mail each day to fulfill my dream of Nirvana. Of course I would win. I was consumed by this thought day and night for weeks. As the time went by, I never heard from Roy Rogers. I couldn't fathom that someone other than me would spend an entire week with him. After several months one Saturday afternoon in the newsreel, I saw the young lady who had won the trip to his ranch. My heart was broken as I saw her riding his horses and smiling in his kitchen. One day the following year my dreams of marrying Roy were thwarted when he married Dale Evans instead.

Eventually Roy was replaced by another idol - Audie Murphy. My passion for him surpassed what I felt for the handsome cowboy. I had to see every movie Audie made and I secretly imagined his arms around me as I basked in his southern drawl and dimpled smile. As the popcorn and candy corn fights subsided, my interest in boys increased. Eventually Audie Murphy's eyes and voice were replaced by the exciting young men who sat next to me in the dark of the theater, struggling with their insecurities, as they decided whether or not to put their arms around me.

Morehouse Influence

Shirley and Carol Morehouse

Hangtown
1934-1940

(Shirley)

My first memories are from the time we lived in Placerville, formerly known as Hangtown. We moved there when I was a toddler and stayed until I was seven years old. In Placerville we lived on Main Street near the old Federated Church. We had a big magnolia tree on each side of the front walk. My mother put the creamy blossoms in a fat blue vase, warning us not to touch the petals or they would turn brown. A big walnut tree in the back housed a tree house where I climbed with my brother and sister and perched unnoticed in the branches. We could see the railroad tracks on the other side of Hangtown Creek beyond our backyard, and we could watch the steam engine working to pick up or drop off railroad cars as it chugged to the fruit packing plant and icehouse just east of us.

My father, well over six feet, was the Presbyterian pastor of the nearby church. He was usually working, only joining his family during the dinner hour. He always wore a dark suit with white shirt and tie. He left the house wearing a gray fedora which he tipped to every lady he met on the

Shirley Morehouse (circa 1935)

sidewalk. I remember the large brick church with a square bell tower. I attended Sunday school in the spacious downstairs room with dark oily smelling wood floors. That is also where we frequently went for potluck suppers, my mother arriving late with us, either with a chocolate cake or a potato salad - we loved both.

On Sundays I climbed a tall staircase with rubber treads, smelling of floor oil to the sanctuary, I held the wooden banister with one hand and my mother's hand with the other. Our family sat on red velvety cushions in the front pew. There, I could look up and see the brass pipes of the organ, the beautiful glass windows and hear Daddy's familiar voice coming from the pulpit. I quietly colored pictures during the service and folded the bulletin into shapes as my brother, Happy, had shown me. Sometimes I fell asleep in my mother's lap.

Carol & Shirley Morehouse (1938)

When I was three my mother had to go to the hospital where she gave birth to my sister, Carol. I remember the young woman who cared for us, would not let us leave the table until we asked to be excused. My brother and sister were excused, but since I was not familiar with that word nor had my mother ever required us to do that, I refused. So I sat at the table and cried. Happy, always the diplomat came to me and suggested it wouldn't hurt me to say the required words. She eventually put me in a crib near the table, which had an unfamiliar cold pink rubber mat with a squared pattern over the mattress. My mother would never have put me on a bare rubber mat. I cried myself to sleep. It was a traumatic experience for me.

I remember helping Happy pick up fragments from the icehouse next to the tracks and we loaded his red wagon. We would pull it home and Mama would put them in the icebox. Sometimes the train engineer would give us a ride in the steam engine down to Hangtown Creek Bridge about a block away. I leaned against his black-stripped knee and Hap blew the whistle. When no one was around Hap scrambled to the top of the railroad cas and walked from one to another. He enjoyed climbing over the railroad trestle as well. The walks into the dry foothills were interesting and fun. There were ghost towns to explore with deserted saloons full of broken mirrors, bottles and chairs, and a number of abandoned mines dotted the area. I remember my sister, Margy, pulling me away from a rattlesnake which was rattling.

Every summer we would go to Lake Tahoe where we would camp and play while Daddy worked at the Conference grounds in Zephyr Cove. We made weekly trips to Sacramento so Happy could have his violin lesson and Margy her piano lesson. My family must have hated traveling with me because I always got carsick during the hour's trip.

Although we lived in Placerville during the depression, we were not much affected by it. My father's salary remained constant, and we continued to get donations such as the weekly pot roast for Sunday dinner with a gallon of neopolitan ice cream. We were aware of the poverty around us when people came to our door for handouts of food, clothes, and blankets. My parents helped people whenever they could, and my mother helped young women with baby clothes and diapers. We made a wide berth around the hotel when we walked to school, because the sidewalk and benches in front of Hangtown Hotel on Main Street were full of men, many of them drunk. The hanging tree was still in the town center and visible from the dentist chair when I had an appointment.

First memories of school were not pleasant. I hated kindergarten and cried every day when my brother and sister left me at class. Then I got sick and stayed that way for most of the next two years. I had red measles first and then whooping cough at the same time. There was a white tent over my bed with a medicinal steamer. But I don't recall whooping or having pain. My brother ran from my room yelling, "She's going to whoop."

I remember lying on the couch watching the family and guests eating in the dining room for several Thanksgiving and Christmas holidays, but I couldn't join them.

I missed first grade and went back to school as a skinny second grader, but I missed so much, I did not know how to read. It was difficult to sit in a reading group and not recognize any words, but I made progress and was soon put into a higher reading group. By the time I reached third grade, I had friends, liked my teacher, and loved to read. And then my family moved.

Margy, Happy, Carol, Shirley

Family Photo
1938

(Shirley)

In the above photo of my brother and sisters, I am standing in front of my brother. My older sister, Margaret, is eleven years old, my brother, Happy, is ten, my younger sister, Carol, is two years, and I am six. Seeing myself with my brother and sisters, brings back the memory of living in a two story brown frame house on Main Street in Placerville. My long curls remind me of how my mother sat me on the floor between her knees every night while she dampened my hair and rolled it up on rag curlers. She read me a story while she worked, and when it was all finished I got a cup of hot ovaltine before going to bed.

In the picture I am in a timid pose. I don't recall being shy, but my sister tells me I was so timid I would constantly hide behind my mother when strangers were near, and be close to tears if someone spoke to me. I pulled my knees back into a locked position, as I am standing in the photo. I don't remember my sister being taller than my brother, but the difference in their height here is dramatic.

87

Shirley Morehouse & Laddie

In a Jam
1941

(Shirley)

I was up early Saturday morning. Everyone in our big household was sleeping except for my Dad who always left for work before 7:00 AM, even on weekends. I thought I would surprise my family and prepare breakfast for everyone, a first experience for me. I felt very self-righteous as I quietly set the table for five and put out juice and cereals. Everything went well until I took a large jar of jam out of the refrigerator. The jar must have been too fat for my small hand, because it slipped and broke on my ankle before spilling to the floor. I remember seeing a slick bluish white dome sticking out of my ankle, which I realized must be bone. My cries brought my family running, and I was whisked away to see Dr. Oakleaf. While he was sewing me up and wrapping my foot, I wondered why I was hurt trying to do something generous and kind for my family. I could understand being hurt if I had done something bad.

My mother prepared a day bed on the screen porch next to the dining room where I could have more company with my solicitous family. I stayed there most of each day for the next week, reading books, playing board games with my brother and sisters and visiting with fourth grade school chums who dropped by to cheer me up. Every evening Daddy carried me upstairs to my bedroom.

When we returned to the doctor to have my stitches removed, the doctor asked, "Why did you keep her in bed? It would have been much better for her to be her usual active self."

Sympathy ended, but the scar is still there.

Harold Geddes Morehouse

Harold's Bio
Born 2/1/1894 - Died 1/20/1945

(Shirley)

My father was born February 1, 1894, the oldest of five boys. Tall and good looking, he measured six feet in the sixth grade, taller than any of the faculty. After he graduated from high school, he enrolled at Humboldt State College in Eureka, where he developed a love for redwood forests and the ocean. Before he graduated, the United States was involved in World War I, and the army recruited him. There he became a staff sergeant and worked as head cook for his unit which was stationed in the Midwest. The war ended in 1919, and his photo album displays shots of the Armistice celebration in Eureka.

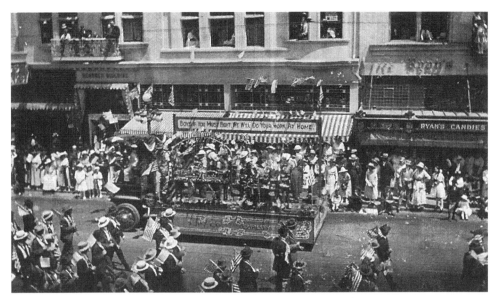

The Armistice celebration in Eureka

Photos of Harold in his bathing suit show him posing with different girls on the beach. He was very popular. It is obvious they found him attractive.

Harold and the Girl He Did Not Marry

After Harold's discharge from the service, he returned to southern California where he intended to enter law school and marry the girl he loved. However, he could not convince her to marry. He dropped out of law school, took the advice of his Scottish grandfather and decided to become a Presbyterian minister. We learned later his girlfriend never married.

Harold enrolled in the San Francisco Theological Seminary at San Anselmo. His grandfather, David Geddes, a pure Scotsman who thought Harold would be a wonderful pastor, influenced him. He moved to Marin County where he began three years of theological training at the Presbyterian Seminary. He enjoyed making friends and was successful in getting to know the professors. Young women, studying Christian education, were also enrolled, but for a shorter time. Some were interested in becoming ministers' wives. Mildred Moore, a pretty, shy, young woman caught Harold's attention. He made a bet with the guys he could get Mildred to go out on a date. He won the bet and that was the beginning of a rapid courtship.

After Harold graduated, he and Mildred were married in the church adjoining the seminary. They moved to his first parish in the countryside Harold most loved - the Pacific Northwest, Scotia, near Garberville. One year after they married, Mildred delivered their first child, Margaret, named after Harold's mother. Eighteen months later they had a son, whom they named Harold Geddes Jr. He soon bore the name Happy because of his sunny disposition. The family moved to Garberville to be closer to the majority of Harold's parishioners and where a new church had been erected. He was popular with the congregation and Mildred said the church was filled every Sunday. Mildred concentrated on her children. She bought an expensive camera and took photos of her family. In 1932 Harold and Mildred had another child, and named her Shirley. When Shirley was two, Harold was asked to move to Placerville to be the pastor of a large federated church.

My first memories of Daddy started when I was three. I remember holding my mother's hand and climbing up the broad staircase with the carved banister to the sanctuary every Sunday. We sat in the front row in a pew with red velvet cushions. I put my head against her and fell asleep.

Daddy took a cold bath every morning. In the winter when the pipes were frozen, shreds of ice would float in his bath water. He was always the first one up and cooked a pot of oatmeal for the whole family before leaving for his office. He was gone long before anyone else was up.

Harold was old fashioned in his family approach. Everyone had his or her own place; the man at the head of the table. His wife was given the same amount of money each month. Mildred always ran out of money and argued with her husband about needing more. This concerned me, and when I was four, I found a blank checkbook, wrapped it, and gave it to them as a gift.

The Placerville Federated Church

     After six years in Placerville, Harold accepted a job as pastor for the Federated Church in Healdsburg. He complained that he had to mediate between Presbyterians and Methodists. In Placerville the problem was how to keep the Methodist and Presbyterian woodpiles separate. In Healdsburg it was how to divide the collection money.

     In Healdsburg the congregation filled the church to capacity to hear him talk. Laughter resonated as he peppered his sermons with jokes. He established a junior choir, which evolved into a popular concert choir some years later. Anyone who enjoyed singing joined that group. Harold worked with youth groups at the Lake Tahoe Conference Center. Our family stayed in a tent at the campgrounds and often ate at the Conference Center. I remember young high school and college students always surrounded him.

Harold Takes a Dip

During the summer of 1940, and the next couple of years my father suffered from a bad heart and high blood pressure. He continued to work too hard. "You must take a vacation," his doctor said. "Your blood pressure is in the stratosphere, and we have to get it down or you will have a heart attack." To make sure he would follow his advice, Dr. Oakleaf arranged for our family to use his oceanfront cabin for two weeks. That was the first and only vacation we ever had. I remember Margy, Happy, and me playing on the beach, after a cold dip. I had never seen my Dad in a bathing suit and didn't know he could swim. He dove through the waves, swam beyond the breakers, and let them wash him to shore I thought. "The ocean is as cold as his bath water at home." We left after just one week because Dad said he must get back to work.

Money problems continually caused stress in our family. My father gave Mom half his salary to pay for food, and all the personal needs for her and the four children. He paid for a new Chrysler, his clothes, travel expenses, and household utilities. Members of the church were generous with donations such as milk and ice cream from the dairy and pot roasts on Sundays from the butcher. However, as I look back, I realize that even though Mildred was a poor manager, she did not have enough money. More than anything else my mother wanted a home of her own with some land, but my father did not. He was content to have the church session provide his housing as it had always done.

When we lived in Healdsburg my father was offered an opportunity to purchase a cabin on the shore of Zephyr Cove from the Presbytery for $50.00. They told him he needed to buy it, as they were not allowed to give it away. He turned that opportunity down. That building today is extremely valuable. When we lived in the Healdsburg Beeson house Dr. Beeson offered to sell it to our family for $1,500 but again, my father turned the opportunity down, as he did not want to own property. Today, the home is registered as one of the famous historical homes of California. Mildred was terribly frustrated by my father's reasoning, but she loved her husband and was proud of him.

When Harold's heart problem went from bad to worse, Dr. Oakleaf put him in the Healdsburg hospital for enforced rest. Smitty, our choir director, worked there as custodian and a number of high school girls who sang in the choir volunteered as nurses's aides. Margy and I were visiting Dad when four to six girls in pink trooped in, stood in line, and kissed Dad good night. He loved it. I was shocked because kissing was something that was never seen in our family, even between my mother and father.

As Harold grew weaker, my mother decided to take him to a doctor in Placerville whom she admired because my father had improved when under his care. I was sitting on the lawn with our collie puppy in my lap. I watched my father reluctantly climb into the back seat with his pillow and Mom drove off.

Shirley and Laddie

When she returned, Daddy, who was in the hospital, sent sad little notes begging us to write to him. He was not allowed to have any visitors and was terribly lonesome. We didn't see those notes until many years later because my mother didn't share them with us. A week later Harold's family was invited to visit and we left right away for Placerville where we stayed with friends. I remember being very cold for I had no coat. We saw Daddy in his hospital room and he held my hand the whole time. I showed him the new pajamas Mommy bought for him. I needed a dress to wear so Mom took me to a store to buy a new one. The only garment they had was too long, so Margy hemmed it up for me after I went to bed. I noticed she was crying as she sewed. The next morning our hosts told us Daddy had died during the night. My mom tried to settle the hospital bill, but was told nothing was owed.

We drove home to Healdsburg after dark. When we arrived our house was lit up, there were flowers everywhere, a fire in the fireplace, a hot dinner on the table, and friends to greet us. My mother was chagrined because her house was not ready for company. The rest of us loved the attention the ladies of the church showed to us.

The cemetery is at the foot of Fitch Mountain next to the golf course. When we reached the gravesite, Margy, Carol, Hap, Mom, and I climbed out of the limousine and joined other relatives along with Dr. Rainer, a pastor friend from the bay area who said a few words I didn't hear. I clutched my gold cross, which was a Christmas gift from Daddy. I couldn't wear it because the chain was hopelessly knotted. I stood next to Aunt Peggy, who gave up trying to untangle the chain. As the first shovel of dirt fell on the coffin, I dissolved into tears, when the finality of never seeing my father again hit me. I felt as if our world had come to an end, and we would be penniless orphans for the rest of our lives.

Harold Morehouse
Alone
1945

(Shirley)

He was lying there in the dark suit and tie, I had seen him wear leaving or coming home from work. Only now he was not going to work any more, nor was he going to laugh, tell jokes, or give me hugs. Different people spoke at the funeral, but I didn't hear what they said. Many people were crying, and the choir sang and then they cried, too. Everyone walked up to look in the casket, and I remember thinking that he looked very handsome and peaceful. I preferred remembering him as I saw him a few days ago while holding his hand next to the hospital bed. No one in our family cried because my mother said it was important for us "to keep our powder dry." During the talks I fantasized about going hungry and being forced to leave our home which was the "manse." Perhaps my unemployed mother would die too, as so often happened in the library books I read about poor struggling orphans.

After the service my mother, brother, and two sisters climbed into a big black Cadillac, which took us to the Healdsburg cemetery. My brother, who sometimes did errands for the funeral parlor, when he was not attending high school, got to drive, and he was pleased at the big adventure. I was relieved to be distracted by his brief pleasure. I was fascinated with the long string of cars following us with no end in sight. We wound up the hill behind the Healdsburg Elementary School where I could see my classmates out at recess on the playground. I wondered if they knew I was in the black car following the hearse.

The cemetery is at the foot of Fitch Mountain next to the golf course. When we reached the gravesite, Margy, Carol, Hap, Mom, and I climbed out of the limousine and joined other relatives along with Dr. Rainer, a pastor friend from the bay area who said a few words I didn't hear. I clutched my gold cross, which was a Christmas gift from Daddy. I couldn't wear it because the chain was hopelessly knotted. I stood next to Aunt Peggy, who gave up trying to untangle the chain.

We stood around my father's grave and watched his body being lowered into the ground. As the first shovel of dirt fell on the coffin, I dissolved into tears when the finality of never seeing my father again hit me. I felt as if our world had come to an end, and we would be penniless orphans for the rest of our lives.

Fifty years later I again stood by the side of my father's grave with my brother and two sisters. The grave had been opened to receive my 94-year-old mother's body. My mother had not married again and struggled ineptly to earn enough money to support her four children. All of the feelings of sorrow and abandonment that I felt at the age of twelve for my father again swept over me. Yet it was accompanied by a feeling of great amazement and gratitude to realize that the four of us not only survived, but had actually done very well, graduating from college, making good marriages, and contributing to the world with our work and our children.

Shirley Morehouse and Laddie

Grandma Moore

Lemon Pie and Sundries
1938-56

(Shirley)

Whenever I devour lemon meringue pie, my favorite, I'm reminded of Grandmother Moore. My memories of visiting Grandma always include a good meal climaxed by her lemon pie; a culinary vision topped with foamy white peaks and valleys, lightly browned, and a tasty lemony filling on soft flaky crust. My three siblings equally appreciated it as we competed for seconds. In our view the pies were worth the long drive from Placerville to Modesto.

On one of our visits when I was four years old, Grandma took me into the front bedroom where an old man was lying in a large bed. "This is your Grandpa," she said. I recall feeling overwhelmed even though Grandpa greeted me kindly. My mother said he had been bedfast for ten years with severe arthritis. He was a doctor, but I guess he couldn't heal himself. We saw him a few more times on infrequent trips. He died when I was six years old and I can barely recall the family gathering for his funeral service.

I remember Grandma's dining room with rich dark wainscoting below the papered walls and a wall clock, which chimed the hours. There was a heavy black chain draped from post to post around

100

the front porch on which I tried to swing, unsuccessfully. A more vivid memory was the intriguing pull chain on the tank above the toilet in the bathroom off the back porch. The first time I yanked on that chain, I was sure disaster had struck. It sounded as if a waterfall was gushing through the ceiling. It was a long time before I had the nerve to flush again. Another scary feature to her house was the cellar. Behind the house, level with the ground, were two wooden doors, which we could lift with a heavy ring, one at a time. When the doors were open we looked into a dark hole accessed by wooden steps. I didn't have nerve to venture into the cellar.

I loved the way Grandmother looked. She wore dresses she knitted herself, which looked classy and trim. Her wavy white hair rolled at her neckline. Her bright sapphire eyes twinkled with humor. Her handiwork was everywhere: all the quilts on the beds, the doilies under lamps and vases, and the lace tablecloth, knit sweaters and socks for everyone. I still use the crocheted potholders she gave me, and Don still wears the socks she knitted for him. Everything was perfectly crafted.

My Grandmother was slight, erect, quick-witted, and she entertained us with poems she could recite from memory with wonderful expression. I especially loved James Whitcomb Riley's "Little Orphan Annie" and the "Raggedy Man" and she started with them. I asked her how she could remember all those poems.

"I have a good memory," she responded, "and I practice memorizing, by learning new poems. For ten years, after I returned from church, I recited the Sunday sermon to my bedfast husband." When I asked what subjects she liked most at school, she said, "I loved math, and astronomy was fascinating. I enjoyed performing in school dramas. Did you know I knew Herbert Hoover in school?"

I'm sure it was hard for Grandma to give up her home and friends in Modesto to live in an upstairs apartment near her son in Berkeley. Later my mother moved Grandma from Berkeley to Placerville, where Mom had space and could better care for her. When Don and I were newlyweds, we visited my mother, and were amazed to find Grandma still memorizing new poems in her late eighties. She died in 1956 at the age of eighty-seven.

Mildred Morehouse: Born 9/12/1899 - Died 1993

A Hard Life

(Shirley)

My mother's family was concerned with cleanliness in a big way. Living with a father who was a medical doctor and a sister who had TB, caused her parents to avoid any contact with harmful germs or bacteria. Dirty dishes were rinsed with boiling water, and sheets and towels were boiled in strong lye solution.

Almost forty years later my mother imposed the same rigorous standards on our family. When everyone else used a washing machine, my mother boiled bedding, towels, pj's, and underwear in a huge boiler on our kitchen range and stirred them with a wooden paddle. I remember the warm steamy smell of soap and lye in the house and film on all the windows. The less active ringer washing machine stood on the back porch.

Mom washed dishes in sudsy water and placed them in a shallow pan and poured boiling over them. We laundered them in stages so the pan could be emptied and dishes dried before more dishes were placed in the pan for a steamy rinse. Then we waited for more water to reach a boiling point in the kettle.

As we grew older my sister and I rebelled against these routines. None of our friends had to sanitize dishes and clothes. Our family was healthy. We bought a dish drainer with rubber mat, which my mother would not use, but we used it on the sly. Now I think of how difficult it must have been for my widowed mother to support four children teaching all day and then dealing with household chores, which included caring for chickens, goats, and pets, along with a big yard. What a Herculean task she had.

Sometimes I think of Mom when my dishwasher, new washing machine, and dryer are slaving away while I am doing what I want to do. I wish she could have had an easier life.

Moving
1940-1950

(Shirley)
First House:

We left Placerville to live in Healdsburg where my father became the pastor of another Federated Church. Our years there turned out to be an exercise in moving. First we lived in a small white stucco house with two bedrooms, a difficult adjustment after the spacious Placerville home. Happy had to sleep in the basement and my mother was worried when she found black widows there. I slept with Margy and my little sister was with my parents. When our grandparents came to visit, we set up a tent in the back yard.

Second & Third Houses:

Our friend, Doc Beeson, offered us the use of his summer guesthouse near Madrona Manor. It backed against an inviting redwood forest. Before summer was over we made another temporary move to a deceased parishioner's furnished home situated on a prune ranch three miles from town. Special memories at this location were riding on a mule in the orchard, and taking a dusty walk to the bank of the Russian River, which formed the eastern boundary to the ranch. There, we splashed around in the swimming hole on hot afternoons. The living room was dated with fringed lampshades and an antique victrola with a flared brass speaker. We cranked it up and played old records, by Enrico Caruso and Marian Anderson, I especially enjoyed the Grand Canyon Suite by Ferde Grofe.

Fourth House:

The Doc Beeson home we were waiting for finally became available, and we moved in. It was beautiful and spacious and located near the library on Matheson Street. It was my mother's dream house, and I never saw her happier. The house had five bedrooms, one for each of us. My sister had a balcony off her room over the front entrance.

A beautiful curved banister staircase of carved mahogany graced the entrance. A window seat with velvety cushions rimmed the hallway beneath a colored glass window. In the back hall off the kitchen, a narrow circular staircase was designed for servants operating the dumb waiter. Fruit trees dominated the back yard. The stable had a wonderful upstairs trap door. There was a carriage portico on the left side of the house where we entered through the screened porch. My mother turned the kitchen breakfast nook into a playhouse for my little sister and me.

I have many special memories of the three years we lived in the big house, During a W.W.II air raid drill; my brother climbed the huge redwood tree alongside our house to see what Healdsburg looked like during a "blackout." My mother was terribly worried when he disappeared, but when she called, she could hear his faraway voice.

The Gilbert family lived cross the street with four kids about our ages. We played croquet, monopoly, listened to the player piano, and drank homemade root beer. At our house we played cops and robbers, touch football, hide and seek, and climbed trees. The overhead trap door in the stable was our secret weapon. The Healdsburg Library a few doors down was a great attraction and I found favorite authors such as Wilder, Alcott, and Dickens. I read everything they wrote. While we lived there, my first love was Laddie, a collie puppy. Earlier we had a kitten that got so much love from my younger sister, Carol, and myself that it did not live beyond a month.

Mary Ann Gibbs and Shirley Morehouse with Pet Dogs (Circa 1942)

Fifth House:

The time came when Doc Beeson said he needed to sell the house. He did not want to put us out, so he offered to sell it for an exceptionally low price - $1,500.00. My father was not interested. He felt it was inappropriate to own property, as the church had always furnished him a home. My mother could hardly stand giving up that house and the wonderful opportunity to buy it, and there were many argumentative discussions in the kitchen. Doc Beeson easily found a buyer who paid $12,000 for his big house. We moved again to a three-bedroom house next door to the Federated Church, a small, rundown, and home with almost no yard. I slept on the porch.

By the time I reached seventh grade, my father was in and out of the Healdsburg hospital. My mother insisted on taking him to her favorite doctor in Placerville where, under his protest, he was placed in the sanitarium where he later died. We drove to Placerville, staying with friends, and were able to visit him shortly before he died. He held my hand and I remember its large size and familiar warmth when we returned home, our house was lit up like a Christmas tree. Food was on the table and a fire blazed in the fireplace. My mother was chagrined that so many people saw our dirty house, but the rest of us were delighted with the homecoming provided by our friends. Mother started looking for another house, and a few months later we moved.

Sixth House

Our home on the Russian River off Fitch Mountain Rd was crowded, but we didn't mind because we had a yard with a beautiful view and our own small pier with a rowboat tied to it. There was a spacious beach across the river with no homes in sight. Margy and Happy graduated from

105

Healdsburg High while we lived in the river house, my mother started teaching in a country school, Carol was in grammar school, and I finished the eighth grade.

The second winter we were there we had severe rainstorms and flooding. I remember the roar of the river kept us awake. One night we heard a loud crash in our back yard. When we investigated in the morning we saw that the retaining wall was gone as well as the steps, the pier, and the boat. We were on a curve of the river and a log or a tree coming down the river hit our bank and wedged behind the wall, tearing everything out. Our basement was flooded which destroyed many boxes of my father's books and sermons stored there.

That did it. My mother said she was putting the house up for sale.

Fitch Mt. House

Seventh House:

Mom always dreamed of living on a farm, and finally, she bought an old rundown farmhouse on four acres. It was located three miles from Healdsburg on Dry Creek Road. I hated the house because it was far from town, and I disliked farming. Mom bought goats and chickens, and put in a vegetable garden. Hap was in charge of the chickens and their house. In addition, we had a barn, a water tower, and an old garage. An orange grove behind the barn provided juicy navel oranges. A picturesque stream spanned by two bridges, flowed through the front lawn, bordered with palm trees.

Mom gave up teaching and cared for a couple of elderly infirm women who boarded with us. She sold doughnuts, eggs, and oranges but we never had enough money. We worked in the fruit harvest every summer. My brother and sister graduated from Santa Rosa Junior College and went to San Francisco State University. My brother barely started before getting drafted during the Korean War. When my sister left home, I had a bedroom to myself until it was taken by one of the boarders. Then, the three of us slept on the porch. It was cold out there, even after Mom had it glassed in.

106

High School went well doing those years. I was very active in a youth fellowship group, a youth choir, and took piano lessons. I was out frequently with friends, and was serious about a boy. Yes, I neglected my first love but he was getting old. My grades were good, but they could have been exceptionally good. Then, my mother decided to sell the house and move back to Placerville to teach.

Alexander Valley House

Eighth, Ninth, and Tenth houses
I was a senior when my mother and Carol left. During that year Hap was discharged from the army and got a job driving a CAT with the logging industry in Willits. Margy was married in Healdsburg to a fellow student from S.F. State and dropped out of college in her senior year to work. Mom made arrangements to have me live with the pastor's family so I could graduate with my class at Healdsburg High. Hap helped pay for my room and board.

I lived with Jack and Evelyn Thomas for the year and helped take care of their boys, three and one years of age. I had my own room upstairs and we lived in the south side of town. That year I settled down, got straight A's, and worked hard with the piano. In the middle of the year the Thomases decided to rent a nicer home on Johnson Street near the hospital. Evelyn was pregnant and expecting in the spring. Shortly after her baby girl was born, the Thomases arranged for me to stay with an elderly couple until I finished school.

107

Graduation drew my years in Healdsburg to a close. For me the highlight of that ceremony was the Etude in G flat by Franz Liszt. I was grateful to get a few good scholarships. Then, I was off to Placerville for the summer where I stayed with Mom and Carol and worked packing pears in the fruit plant the summer before entering college.

Jack & Evelyn Thomas

Hap With One of His Many Cars

A Surprise
1944

(Shirley)

"How about helping me clean up the rowboat?" Hap suggests as we look forward to coming spring activities. I enjoy being with my big brother, so I readily agree. Hap, now a senior in High School is five years ahead of me.

We gather up some rags and walk down the sloping lawn to our rickety wooden stairs leading down the steep bank to the Russian River. The rowboat is tied to the side of a small wobbly pier. Our property, situated on a curve of the river provides deep water good for swimming, and a fast current. Directly across from us a spacious rocky beach connects to shallow water.

"We better go to the other side where we can pull the boat up on the beach," Hap observes. We untie the boat, step in and I take a seat to gather up the oars. Hap balances in the boat as he lifts a low overhanging branch, which is impeding our progress. As he lifts the branch with both hands, the swift current takes the boat out from under him, and I am headed downstream, working helplessly with the oars.

"Row back" Hap calls, legs flailing. I see him looking at me bumbling with the oars, and watch a flicker of resignation cross his face as he drops into the water, shoes first. I am laughing so hard I'm doubled over the oars. It took me awhile to collect enough energy to row to the shallow side of the river where a dripping wet brother waited for me.

Fortunately, he was not angry but rather chagrined by his lack of judgment and just anxious to return to our house to warm up and put on some dry clothes.

109

In the deep water behind our house, I finally learned to swim and when the current caught me and swept me over the holes, I frantically dog paddled to the shallower water.
From then on I no longer feared the deep places in the river.

Margy, Shirley, Happy, Carol at Lake Tahoe (Circa 1937)

Charles McCord

A Gift
1947-50

(Shirley)

When we moved to Healdsburg my sister and brother continued their music lessons for piano and violin respectively. They took them from Mr. and Mrs. McCord, but my younger sister and I did not get this option as my parents could not afford more musical instruction. I listened to Margy playing beautiful pieces, and I copied the tunes by ear. Margy heard me struggling to find the right notes and showed me how to figure out their names. I was about to enter High School when Mrs. McCord came to our house and heard me playing *The Moonlight Sonata*. She said to my mother: "Do you mean to tell me that Shirley can play like that and she has never had lessons? I will be happy to give her instruction for no charge." My life was changed.

I stepped off the Healdsburg H.S. bus and walked to a Victorian farmhouse on West Matheson Street. I looked forward to my weekly piano lessons with Frances McCord. I climbed the steps to the spacious curved porch and turned the bell knob. Mrs. McCord answered the door with a wide smile, her blue eyes snapping, and her flyaway reddish blond hair unsuccessfully tied back.

"Hi Shirley, come in, come in," She motioned me to the piano bench of the large upright. I detected fried liver smells coming from the swinging door and could hear Mr. McCord clearing dishes while he listened to the popular conservative commentator, Gabriel Heater, on the radio. The spacious living room with its creaky wooden plank floors, magazines and newspapers, stacks of music, and stands attested to the lifestyle of two busy teachers.

I have some new music for you. You'll enjoy this Warsaw Concerto, and these two are pretty difficult. I'll play some of each, and you tell me which one you like best." She played a Chopin piece, which went like the wind, and an Etude by Franz Liszt which started with beautiful running arpeggios. I chose the Liszt.

I was beginning my senior year and, after three years of piano lessons with Frances McCord, had developed a good repertoire of classical of music. I practiced the Liszt for a whole year and played it for my High School graduation.

The McCords were important during my high school years. Late on a moonlit summer night we finished choir practice and decided to serenade special friends. "We have to sing for Mr. & Mrs. McCord," I insisted. So we piled into the back of Frosty's pickup and my brother's Buick convertible, and silently parked near the McCord's. We crept up to the side of the house and sang *Tell Me Why* and *Let Me Call You Sweetheart*. I tried to do a perfect job singing the soprano obligato but I messed up the opening. The McCords came out on their porch to listen, arm in arm, silhouetted against the lighted window.

The McCords invited me to go to the opera in San Francisco and I was amazed to see their second home, in pristine white stucco with a bay window looking out on the Marina and a courtyard garden in the middle of the house. My bedroom had a satin spread with a stiff bolster roll. This was a new experience. The opera house was a delight, as was my first opera, *Lohengrin*. Whenever I hear the famous prelude to the third act, I can visualize the entire scene.

On the day after graduation, I had a piano lesson with Mrs. McCord. After the lesson she gave me a card, which I opened, nervously reading the message, and glancing at a check for $1.00 made out to me. When I got home I looked again at the check and saw it was a check for $100.00, not $1.00. I rode my bike back to the McCord's and Mrs. McCord said, "I thought you read the check wrong. Give Mr. McCord a kiss."

I had never kissed another adult, not even my mother or father. I gave each of them an awkward kiss, but I'm sure they knew how much I appreciated the gift.

Because of the McCords, music became an important part of my life. The lessons allowed me to minor in music, accompany choirs, play in musical groups, and play the local church organ. The money encouraged me to start college at San Jose State, which cost $7.00 a semester, rather than at Santa Rosa Junior College which was free.

A Graduation Present
1944

(Shirley)

It was a big night for the eighth grade class as the students gathered in the new gymnasium of Healdsburg Elementary School. I was expected to give a memorized speech with the aid of a microphone. I was chosen because Mrs. Luce, my English teacher, chose me because she liked the essay I wrote in her class.

My mother had added a paragraph expressing her opinion about church music, which she had copied from a favorite magazine and I dutifully memorized it. After the ceremony one of my father's friends greeted me, "Your mother wrote your speech, didn't she?' I was embarrassed to admit it was true.

He asked me "Would you like to be a teacher, a secretary, or maybe a nurse?"
I was dismayed by so few options and responded, "I would like to run an orphanage."
After the program, the auditorium was cleared so the students could dance.
I knew nothing about dancing and was reluctant to show my ignorance.
My brother Hap, who had just graduated was there with a friend. They offered to take me to the soda

fountain at the local pharmacy for a graduation treat and I jumped at the chance. I could vividly remember watching the soda jerk at Tomasco's Drug Store prepare a strawberry soda or concoct a banana split, sauce dripping over the strawberry ice cream and hot fudge smeared over the chocolate ice cream. It was my first date.

Outside, Hap pulled open the rumble seat of his Buick coupe. My older sister, Margy, rode in the front with Hap. Kirk and I eased our selves into the back, using the step on the fender before dropping onto the welcoming leather cushions. We drove through town and parked at the Central Plaza Park opposite Tomasco's. I already knew Kirk from seeing him at school in the class ahead of me, and was one of his admirers. Kirk and I snuggled up and he held my hand as we drove through town. and I thought that was pretty good. The banana split was delicious and a memorable graduation gift.

Kirk and Shirley

The Garage Fire
1946

(Shirley)

"Remember, the fire extinguisher will always be right here, and we'll use it if there is any kind of fire."

Mom, then a widow, impressed this on each of us while pointing to the bright cylinder she hung on our back porch. She got quite a scare when my younger sister, Carol, caught her pajamas on fire standing too close to the kitchen stove. Fortunately, Carol was smart enough to roll into the nearby ironing basket to smother the flame, but not without getting painful burns.

We lived in an old frame farmhouse on Dry Creek road several miles from Healdsburg, and our property included huge palm trees around the house, as well as a separate two car garage, a red barn, a storage shed, a chicken house, and a tank house. The danger of fire never occurred to us, but I am sure it was on Mom's mind. I recall her hoeing the high dry weeds along busy Dry Creek Road, trying to make a fire break between the traffic and our property.

My eighteen-year-old brother was infatuated with cars and motors, and when he was not attending Santa Rosa Junior College, he often worked on his car, Mom's car, or the motor scooter, his friend, Wayne Brown, left at our house when he joined the navy.

It was Christmas Day when Hap returned to our garage after a motor scooter ride. He was trying to replenish the depleted gas tank when the hot cylinder burst into flames. He ran to the house, and got the fire extinguisher from the back porch. When he returned to the garage, he found the motor scooter engulfed in flames along with the dry oil soaked garage floor. Because the ground sloped under the garage floor, outside air force fed the blaze and flames shot up the walls. The old wooden structure was beyond saving with the fire extinguisher.

Hap called the Healdsburg Fire Department and hosed the house roof and sparking areas near the house. Mom made decisions about what items to save, and my older sister and I helped her carry possessions to the front lawn. I heard my little sister crying down the road, but no one took time to find and comfort her. We were faced with the imminent danger of losing everything. I wasn't frightened but thought, *so this is what it is like to have a fire.* I did not believe we would lose our house.

The Fire Department arrived shortly, and by the time they put out the flames, we completely lost the garage, part of the tank house, suffered damage to a couple of trees, but our home was saved.

In the midst of the excitement, I remember getting a call from my high school boy friend, Kirk, inviting my older brother, sister, and me to a movie. I used the old phone attached to the dining room wall with a crank coming out of the wooden box, which allowed six or seven parties to use the same line. Breathlessly, I told him, (and probably our neighbors), of the fire in progress. Kirk and his friend, Rob, came right out. We stood around and watched the excitement and they helped us carry everything back into the house. Afterward, Kirk, Rob, my sister, brother, and I went to the movie in town.

I remember my Mom saying, "You're going to a movie? But we just had a fire."

Later that evening my brother said "I wonder why I never thought to move the scooter out of the garage."

Happy at Sixteen

116

The Gang in Frosty's Truck

A Close Call
1947-49

(Shirley)

I look at my teen-age years, and think of many interesting adventures I had with my friends, which from an adult perspective, makes my skin crawl.

I was in a group of ten to fourteen high schoolers that enjoyed playing at Russian River beaches near Healdsburg, biking in Alexander Valley, climbing Fitch Mountain, and driving to the Coast or San Francisco. Most of our group sang in the Federated Church Youth Choir each Sunday. Occasionally we performed concerts locally or in the Bay Area. Don Frost or Frosty as we knew him, drove a pickup, and as many as ten kids could fit in the bed. It was made more comfortable with a bed of hay and some blankets. Often we overflowed into my brother's convertible or David Gilbert's 1936 Plymouth.

One wintry weekend day, Frosty with other friends turned into our drive. "Hey, there's fresh snow up on Mt. St. Helena. Let's go!" they called.

My older brother and sister and I readily agreed and we grabbed our wraps and piled into the back of the truck. We drove to David's house and he agreed to join us. Dave got into his car and took six passengers from the crowded pickup. We drove to the snowy peak, threw missiles at each other, talked to the ranger at the lookout tower, and played with a mysterious jar of mercury, which had been mined in the vicinity. Later, in college I learned it was dangerous to roll mercury around in your hands.

As we descended the mountain I was in the back seat of David's car with five other passengers, doubled up, sitting in laps. Everything was fine until the car's brakes gave out. We took the next big turn too fast and knew we were in big trouble. We headed over a steep cliff and crashed into a tree. The side of the car was crumpled and the door was gone. David was missing from the driver's seat. I remember the bizarre feeling of watching Dave running along the edge of the road before we left him behind. Dick Pierce, sitting in the front seat, reached across Alberta and grabbed the wheel. He steered the car into the bank on the other side of the road. The car scrapped along the hillside until he managed to bring it to a halt, using the emergency brake. Frosty stopped the pickup behind us and yelled, "What happened? I came around the turn and found David running down the road."

Our group piled into the pickup and managed to make it down from the mountain safely. Once back in Healdsburg, we took the Fitch Mountain girls home first, explaining to the parents what happened. The parents seemed to be more amazed and alarmed than I remember feeling. David's car was out of commission and he was relieved from driving for a while, but we continued to ride around in the back of Frosty's truck.

We went to San Francisco to see a matinee of Madame Butterfly in the Opera House. . During the opera we noticed a number of the boxes were unoccupied and we took the liberty of changing our seats, enjoying the performance from a different perspective. We spent the night in a youth hostel next to the Westminster Church where my sister, Margy worked and lived while attending S.F. State University at the downtown campus. The girls slept in a dorm room.

In the wee hours of the morning a massive explosion that sounded like a cannon in our room awakened us. The girls woke screaming. Rob Pierce, a chemistry student at Cal had dropped a large piece of sodium into a tub of water outside the window. Luckily, it did not cause damage, and no one was hurt. It was a mystery to me that the police did not come to investigate.

Another time when some of us were attending Choir School at the San Francisco Theological Seminary on the hill in central San Anselmo, we climbed into the tower and set off fireworks. It is fortunate we didn't burn that lovely historical building down.

Our children did not seem to have the same opportunities to get into trouble; at least I don't think they did.

Don Frost, the Musician

A Thoughtful Hap

Hap Finds A Way
1950

(Shirley)

A familiar old Buick convertible came towards us as we were driving home on Hwy 101 to Healdsburg. The driver's face, bare arms, and clothes were the shade of mocha chocolate, but his flowing hair was white as the teeth in his smile when he passed. When I recognized him enough to wave, I told my driver, "That's Hap, my big brother. He's coming home from his logging camp in Willits. Most of the time he operates the cat.

I arrived home to find a dejected Hap holding an official letter from the draft board. He'd been drafted and ordered to report for duty. He left San Francisco State College where he was a music major to take the logging job to make enough money to finish his education. In a short time he was off to boot camp and I headed to San Jose State College.

The next time I saw him he was looking forward to going to Germany. He shared some of his basic training experiences. He hated the outdated class system in the army. For some reason the sergeant position attracted men who were brutal, ruthless, and unreasonable. Hap discerned the musicians were better off than the struggling recruits, who endured rigorous exercises and marches every day while the army band provided a brisk rhythm. Hap, an accomplished violinist, asked the band director if he could use another musician.

"Can you play the bass drum?" asked the director. " Sure." Hap had never touched one.

During calisthenics and marches Hap played the drum. He marched at the rear of the band and his function was to maintain the cadence. His problem was he couldn't allow for the time it took to swing the drumstick so that the beat of the drum would match the feet of the marchers as they hit the ground. It took a while to adjust.

Hap discovered that playing the bass drum was more difficult than he realized. When he left the army, he took up the violin again. Today he plays in the Reno Symphony.

Suzy & Hap

Hap & Suzy

Everyone Seems Normal
1928-present

(Shirley)

Brother Bob Kirkpatrick gifted us with a ceramic plaque and hung it over our back entrance. It reads, "Everyone seems normal until you get to know them." How true. After getting to know a person well, I often discover how unique he seems. This is especially true of my brother Harold.

Hap (Harold only on his birth certificate) lives in Washoe Valley near Reno and defies any label. He appears to be a true mountain man with his blond beard, cowboy boots, and hat, driving an old pickup and toting a hunting rifle. I have watched him sitting on a fence conversing easily with a group of cowboys.

Hap wears a suit when he works at the University of Nevada as Dean of the Libraries, and lectures to graduate classes. He is a true academic, now partially retired. He appears at the Performing Arts Center, wearing a dark suit, a talented musician carrying his violin to the symphony concerts. After two failed marriages, Hap lives alone in his rustic cabin at the base of a 12,000-foot

121

mountain, which he climbed on his 75th birthday. Hap has a partner, Suzy, who is also a professional librarian. Suzy lives in her contemporary home in Reno.

Hap's home is as unique as its owner. His living room contains a ping-pong table, a huge stone fireplace, and a stereo system with a shelf full of classical CDs, a stuffed cubbyhole desk, and a floor-to-ceiling beer can collection. There is a chopping block in the dining room next to a wood stove. Water comes from a mountain stream, which is diverted to flow under the house, into the pond in front and through the garden before continuing down the slope.

Nearby in a sagebrush field sit a Porsche, a carryall, a pickup, a station wagon and a Lincoln sedan - all antiques except the Lincoln. There is no garage, but some vehicles are covered.

Hap and Suzy enjoy wandering the world together. They have visited Peru, Iceland, The Isle of Man, and they explored Panama before traveling the canal. Hap, always infatuated with the Queen Mary II, booked a voyage to England on her Majesty's ship, followed by a January trip to Chicago to show Suzy what cold weather is really like. He rafted through the Grand Canyon, and would have climbed Kilimanjaro if he hadn't needed a knee replacement. When he was younger before it was made illegal, he climbed to the top of the Golden Gate Bridge a few times at night.

Hap comes to the coast where he climbs ocean bluffs, pausing to study wave patterns, rock formations, and wildlife behavior. He sits at our kitchen table in the pop-out window working the latest NY Times crossword puzzle (in ink) while drinking a beer. His conversation jumps from humor to astute observations about politics or world issues. He is always interested and supportive of his listeners. When they visit, he and Suzy continually look for another great hike and a fine dining experience, where Hap will order the perfect wine to accompany a wonderful meal.

I feel fortunate to have Hap for a brother, and am pleased he cannot be characterized as "normal."

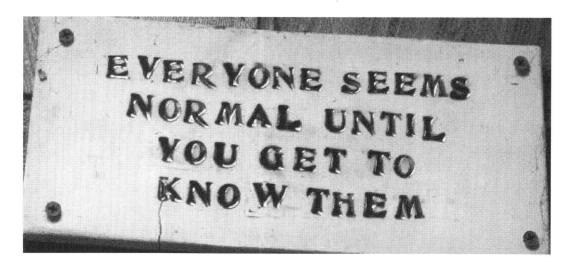

The Mountain House

1950-54

Betty, Ilma, Newt, Shirley at Camp Rose House

The Camp Rose House
1950-54

(Don)

Our father built the house at Camp Rose in 1937 as his first "real job" following a two-year stint of working for the government herding a W.P.A crew. The original owner of the property is unknown but when it came on the market some thirteen years later our parents decided to buy it. Coming out of the recession of the thirties Kirk and Ilma were scraping the bottom of the money barrel but Kirk had a few shekels squirreled away and they decided to take a chance. Pop knew the property well and had built the two rental cabins, which helped to pay the mortgage.

The year after I graduated from Healdsburg High School our family moved to the Camp Rose house on the Russian River. On weekends Bob and I visited with our college friends to ogle the girls.

The house became our beach party playground.

(Betty)

I remember that place quite clearly. We moved in 1950 when I was ten. One drove by the little county store, and summer cabins down the road, which dipped past the rocky beach. On the left were a few summer homes, occupied three to four months of the year. Pop built the house years earlier and Mom hated it the moment we moved in. I knew immediately when I saw the inside of the house there would be trouble. Its dim interior was covered with dark knotty pine walls. The living room featured a gigantic fireplace made of huge river stones but the kitchen was tiny. A big porch extended the full length of the house and overlooked the river. The entire house emitted an aura of gloom and depression, which I could feel and smell. At first Mom and Pop occupied the front bedroom downstairs but Mom eventually moved to the back bedroom by herself. Not a week went by that she didn't complain about its gloominess to Pop and storm about – upset at this new living situation.

There were two bedrooms upstairs with slanted ceilings giving one a closed in feeling of living in an attic. The large room between the bedrooms was a storage area. My bedroom was a small one on the left at the top of the stairs, and Bob and Don were on the right - past the stairs. In the summer bullfrogs croaked so loud the noise kept me awake.

In the Winter Mom was unbelievably paranoid. She screamed constantly. Most of the arguments were over the thermostat. Mom liked the house hot, and Pop wanted it cooler. Mom turned it up to 85 or 90 degrees and Pop turned it down to 70. Mom cranked up the temperature just to annoy my father, for the house was unbearably hot. In the winter when the weather cooled, Pop put a sheet of plywood over the stairs and closed off the top half of the house to conserve heat. This meant I had to sleep in the back bedroom with Mom in the other single bed. I hated it because I couldn't escape her temper tantrums. When she was in her agitated state, she woke in the middle of the night, shook me, and screamed. My sleep was affected and I often had nightmares. I lived in fear of her temper.

Steep steps led to the house from the beach, and steeper steps carved into the hill behind and climbed to the road above. In good weather we ate on the porch, overlooking the river. There was a nest of yellow jackets living near that corner and while we sat at the table, Pop would simply slap his hands and kill them. I became adept at doing the same thing, but one day was cured of that skill when the yellow jacket stung me.

The house had a long porch with a sweeping view of the river and a small sandy spot of beach in front. Early every morning in the summer we had to run down and plant a big blue and white striped umbrella to stop people from camping out there. The beach was composed mostly of big rocks, which were difficult to walk over. At the bend a rope was tied in a tall tree so the more daring swimmers could swing far over the river. I was never allowed to go on it and I couldn't sneak a swing, because it was beyond my grasp.

125

(Bob)

At the far end of the beach the river curved and made a swimming hole, which was a major attraction for Healdsburg teenagers. Each year the current at the apex of the bend scooped the sand out of a large hole and kept the spot swim able and usually deep enough to permit diving from the bank on the far side. The local daredevils attached a rope high in a tree and on summer days Tarzan could be heard calling to Jane. The trick was not to let go of the rope at the wrong time because one could bounce a bottom in the shallows on the out swing or crack a head on the return. Dare deviling reached its peak in 1950 when Johnny Hassenzahl, who had been a star athlete at Healdsburg High School, climbed the rope and dove forty feet from the top of the tree. He misjudged his dive, hit the rocky bottom and broke his neck. Johnny spent the rest of his life in a wheelchair.

The Fearsome Rope Swing

(Betty)

One of my joys was to roam the hills behind our house. During the winter I explored the yards around empty houses on the river waiting for the return of the laughter and sunshine, summer would bring. In the autumn, I climbed the slopes and sat among oak and manzanita trees. The sweet fragrance of the drying leaves evoked peace and solitude. The sun on my skin soothed me when I was in pain. I left my private hideaway feeling centered and healed. I picked Indian Paint brush and Hens and Chickens on the hills and brought them home to press in a book, hoping that the memory and peace of the day would seep through the pages and stay with me.

In the wintertime the river rose, angry and swollen, and roared past the house like a freight train - the muddy brown water crept slowly up the driveway until it extended its fingers into our garage, prying boxes loose and attempting to carry away anything that was not on high shelves. The river swept huge trees and logs along and I was fearful of the current's rapid passage, convinced I might be swept away. Every year it washed over the road and we had to park our car on higher ground at the Camp Rose Store I had a little brown dog-named "Dushka" ("darling" in Russian) who wandered too near the rising flood one winter, and disappeared. I was devastated and tried not to think how it happened. I simply erased it from my mind.

Betty and Dushka

(Bob)

The wide covered porch which ran the length of the house commanded a sweeping view of the swollen Russian River in the winter of a wet year. Once when the water actually came into our garage and Mom was stressed beyond the breaking point. We kids thought it was exciting to see whole trees float by. We watched as a half sunken chicken house with a rooster perched on the apex of the roof disappear around the bend.

There were three houses on the property. A small one-bedroom cabin was rented to Jim Thomas, who taught with Mom in Windsor. The other cabin was larger with two floors. It was our job to clean the houses after the summer tenants left. We scrubbed the floors, scoured the stove and carried away a mountain of garbage. In the evenings we sat in the front yard and played canasta. I was introduced to a new game I had never heard of – strip poker. It was fun because I never lost enough to cause embarrassment. I learned to put on extra shirts and socks and load my hair with bobby pins before we played. When one boy got down to the essentials, he quit before he had to remove his pants.

I had a gray cat, which followed me from North Street where it was a kitten and it now lived outside and slept in the garage. My brother, Bob, named it *Cookie* because it came from a litter belonging to the baker at the Home Bakery. I loved *Cookie* but as it got older, it became cantankerous and didn't like anyone but me. One year someone must have shot it for it showed up with a BB hole in the side of its head. He survived that injury, but that winter it simply disappeared.

My canary, *Tweety Bird,* which I brought from West Grant Street was my joy. When I walked home, I filled my pocket with chickweed for the bird. I had a bird bathtub and bought a cuttle bone for him to sharpen his beak. At his North Street house, John Aikaa taught me how to talk to the bird and coax it to eat out of my hand by holding the chickweed through the bars. As Manda was cooking dinner, he sat for hours talking to the bird until it became quite tame. When we lived on North Street a second time several years later, I was devastated when a cat managed to get in the back door of the duplex and inside the cage. Tweety Bird was no more.

(Don)

One summer morning shortly after the fourth of July, Bob came up with a spectacular way of using left over fireworks. He said "Let's get that old artillery shell that Onnie gave us in the box of junk last Christmas, I have an idea." We buried the casing in the beach up to its rim and put a firecracker in it to see what would happen. After a few lightweight "whoomps," He said: "Let's try something different. Don, go get a tennis ball from the box under my bed." We set the tennis ball on top of the rim holding the fuse in place and lit the cherry bomb. After a few seconds it stopped smoking. "Drat, he said "It's gone out." and he started to walk toward the shell. But a thunderous explosion shook the ground and the tennis ball became a speck in the sky, almost disappearing from sight. We stood there with open mouths. Bob said "That ... was ... *awesome.*" When recovered, one half of the ball was still smoking and scorched to the rubber. "We'd better get out of here before the police come." I agreed. All these years later I do not feel guilty about taking that tennis ball downtown and throwing it into the High School tennis court. I can imagine the puzzled conversation it must have caused.

(Betty)

I was excited during the holidays because Bob and Don came home then and Mom would be on her best behavior. Bob always brought a different girl. Some were terrific and others were only OK. In 1952 Mom and Pop celebrated their 25th anniversary with a party. I didn't know they had so many friends.

Bob Kirkpatrick & Jackie Penzotti.

(Betty)

On occasion I walked a mile up the road to the *Del Rio Woods* skating rink. I loved the huge building with its dark interior. We skated around the rink, flirting with the boys or competing in speed. The electric organ droned, and I could hum *Nola* in my sleep. When *Good Night Irene* was played, it triggered a collective sigh of disappointment because it signaled the end of the evening.

For a few brief months, I had crush on Cullen Wilder who lived at *Mirabel,* but later it was his mother I stopped to see. She was creative and funny with a smile on her face and delighted to see me. There were always cookies in the jar waiting to be devoured. For years after I left Healdsburg, I visited her when I was in town.

I preferred swimming at *Mirabel* because the beach wasn't as rocky as the *Camp Rose beach* and a small dam made the water deeper. There were more friends there and we had good time swimming to the large square raft with a diving board. The boys hollered, jumped, and "cannon balled" the girls.

One day we played underwater tag and I swam too near the dam. I was sucked into the swift current and pulled toward the dam. Caught and terrified, I thought I would drown, but with prayer and a superhuman effort, I pulled myself to the surface. Choking and spitting, I swam frantically to the shore. I never told anyone of that experience for I was positive I would be forbidden to swim there again.

*

I climbed the stairs built into the hill behind the house in order to catch the school bus. It was a steep climb but at the top, the view of the river was spectacular. The green ribbon of water curved past the beach far below, hidden by feathery cottonwood trees. In the summer evenings the sound of bullfrogs filled the air.

We had a large stand of bamboo growing along our drive between the beach and our house. One year Mom decided the "damned bamboo." must be cut down. She kept after Pop for days until he relented and worked for a week hacking it. We could see the beach from our property but our house was now bare and exposed. Less than two weeks passed and the bamboo began to shoot up again. Soon it was back to where it had been before. The lush green vegetation acted as a screen to protect our property from prying eyes. Secretly, I was delighted. In spite of Mom's ranting, the bamboo had a mind of its own and would not be cowed by her.

There was a patch of sand in front of the house, which was a delightful place to be. Early in the morning on summer days we raced to the spot and put up our umbrella. When we didn't, tourists who stayed at Camp Rose would ensconce themselves there with their beach towels. They played loud radios and left trash in our front yard. I sat on our beach towel in the afternoon with my new spaniel, Corky, and corrected papers for Mom.

Betty and Corky
(Don)

The first time Shirley and I made love was in the summer of 1951. We had watched Humphrey Bogart fall in love with Lauren Bacall in *The Big Sleep* for the second time. And were looking for a place to park. The movie finished early and Shirley's mother wasn't expecting her home quite yet. The moon was full and we decided the Camp Rose beach would be a good place to watch it glide across the sky. It was cold and I suggested that one of the empty cabins would be cozier. We crawled into the bed to get warm and that we did. Now more than sixty years later, I remember the event as one glorious day. In the fall of 1952, Shirley and I had an engagement party at the Camp Rose house and in February of 1953, we were married at the Federated Church in Healdsburg.

Betty Kirkpatrick, Dick Gardella and Diane Wolking enjoy the beach.

Picking Prunes
1950

(Betty)

It was difficult to earn money as a kid in Healdsburg, until I discovered picking prunes could be lucrative. I was ten when Jeannie Oak leaf and I picked together - competing to see who could pick the most. I hated the first and last cleaning of the trees for the prunes were sparse and you had to carry the large oil can bucket many rows to fill a box. But when the prunes were ripe, the shaker hooked a long pole over the branches and shook the purple fruit hanging on the stems. The good shakers could manage to rattle the ripe prunes while leaving the green fruit still on the trees. I appreciated that because picking was easier and cleaner.

The ground was covered with a thick purple carpet as far as the eye could see; it transformed the orchard into a wonderland. If you knelt when you picked, your knees got bruised and painful, so

I learned to bend from my waist and swing back and forth sweeping up the prunes as fast as I could and fling them into the bucket. This process could fill a bucket in record time. I didn't like picking in the small bucket, because it took four buckets to fill the fifty-pound boxes that grew in stacks at the end of the rows. It wasted time walking that far. I opted for the larger round oilcan, which required only two trips to the boxes. I started on the side of the tree closest to the boxes and worked my way down the row bent over like a vacuum machine. When noon came, it was difficult to straighten up. By five o-clock every muscle and bone in my body screamed at me.

I loved Imperial prunes as they were larger and it took fewer to fill a box. We often picked directly onto the large drying trays. You could cover those quickly and there was a five -cent premium for a filled one.

I staked out my competition early so I could gauge how fast to go. I usually won by a box or two, until one day when Mr. Fallen hired a group of migrant workers in midseason. I picked in the row next to the family and calculated it was the father I had to compete with. I never saw anyone pick as fast as that man. The fruit flew off the ground into his pail. His hands scooped masses of fruit into the large bucket and he left me in the dust.

The second and third days were the hardest on the body. The muscles cried out in protest as I began in the cold dawn, and bent to pick again. On those days I gave in and knelt to pick on my hands and knees. Wobbly legged, I counted up the boxes at the end of the day - a bad day was three dollars. Once, after picking as fast as I could, I proudly earned ten dollars. I never topped that. With what I earned I went to Spouse-Ritz and bought a large green and white striped beach towel. It cost nine dollars and was the first item I bought with my own money.

Mr. Fallen had an old truck he drove up and down the rows as he checked on us and gathered the boxes to take to the dryer. He was in his nineties and loved to floor the old truck to make it go fast. His foreman, at the pleading of Mr. Fallen's family, put a governor on the accelerator so that it couldn't go faster than fifteen miles an hour. You could hear the motor as it revved up, with curses emanating from the cab as the truck moved slowly down the rows. He never found out what was wrong with his truck.

One year our church youth group decided to pick prunes to raise money for a charity. We set out on the back of an old truck, singing *Kumbaya, 100 Bottles of Bee*r and harmonizing on *The Old Oaken Bucket*. After a half hour drive, we arrived at the orchard and I was disappointed to see we were at the "first picking" which meant a long, difficult day cleaning the ground with few prunes for the effort. Jeannie Oakleaf was my competition and we tried to outdo each other. The price my body paid at the end of the day was enormous. My legs were wobblier than usual, and had no strength as we rode back on the truck, but my spirit soared. What a wonderful time we had picking for the homeless. Knowing that we had done something special for someone else was a new and exhilarating experience.

Going home we didn't sing as much as we did going out, as we were completely exhausted. The truck pulled up at the church and all the mothers and fathers picked up their kids - except mine. I sat and waited for almost an hour until Jack Thomas, the minister came by to offer me a ride. Feeling teary, I refused and he offered to call my home. He unlocked the church and made the phone call. When he returned he said, "Your mother said to begin walking and she would pick you up."

The distance from the church to our home around Fitch Mountain was several miles on a curvy two-lane road with no room at the side for a pedestrian to walk. As I started I could hardly move. My legs trembled and I was covered with dirt and sweat. I hoped Mom would come soon. I kept scanning the cars but hers wasn't there. I reached the outskirts of the city and began the hilly road around the mountain. I became more discouraged with each passing car. The late afternoon sun beat down on me and the grime and dirt on my face and neck began to drip down my shirt in rivulets. I wiped my neck and face, and needed a drink of water badly. My shoes were like two lead weights. One or two cars stopped to offer me a ride.

"Betty, want a lift?"

"No, I'm waiting for my Mom to come."

After time passed and as I continued to walk, I realized she wasn't coming and began to cry. I must have been a sight trudging along the dry grass, grimy, sweaty, red faced. Another sensation began to grow - the familiar "sick to my stomach" knot that often gave way to overwhelming fear. What was the problem? Why was she punishing me this way? Often the uncontrolled anger was over a small, imagined infraction or it was completely irrational. Which was this? I searched my mind for anything that had been a problem. What sort of physical abuse was ahead? Those last terrible miles were a mixture of dread, fear and exhaustion.

When I arrived home, I climbed the steep steps and spied the car in the garage. She had never left to get me. "There you are," she screamed as I opened the door. "It took you long enough to get home."

Puzzled and hurt I replied, "You told the minister that you were picking me up."

"Harrumph – Why didn't that little smartly Jeannie Oakleaf bring you home? She arranged this."

"But you said you were coming."

Ignoring me, she began to hit me with the large wooden spoon she was holding. "You are never to pick prunes for the church again. You shouldn't be giving your time and energy to them. You should be earning the money for yourself. Call her right now and tell her you are not going to pick for the youth group any more."

I called Jeannie and tried to keep myself from crying as I explained I couldn't pick prunes for the church any more, all the while my mother was standing next to me to make sure I didn't tell her the reason. She threw the rag she was holding at me "get in there and scrub that kitchen floor." Almost fainting from exhaustion and hunger I got down on my knees and began to wash, dipping the rag into the bucket and carefully wringing it out. I feared that she would beat me on the head as I was bent over, but she grabbed her keys and slammed the door as she left. I was grateful for the hiatus and later sighed in relief as I lowered my painful body into the warm tub. Mom never came home that night until after I was asleep.

College Days

1949-54

The Duplex at 401 & 403 North Street

The Summer of 1950
1950

(Don)

After the learning experience of the summer of '49, I was understandably wary of using my hard earned college savings for anything but paying rent at Berkeley and perhaps for taking out girls. Nevertheless, the next summer, my indomitable brother, came up with another scheme for pooling resources and making money. Our father was not in the position to employ us for a summer job, but he was willing to let us have an empty lot, which was part of a larger parcel he owned in the middle of town. The prune orchard was removed and it was a prime building lot fronting on North Street. We could sell the lot, put the money into our separate college bank accounts and spend time on the beach at Camp Rose or we could learn more about the construction trade by building a house on it. It was our father's way of teaching us about making choices we would face in our lives.

Bob, having learned nothing from our previous twelve hour, seven day at fifty cents an hour summer, advocated for building because an empty lot wouldn't earn us much money and we both agreed that a summer job made sense.

(Bob)

We thought a duplex was the way to go because each of us would then own a house. Our father drew up the plans and helped us walk them through the City Building Department. Once again we cleaned out our savings accounts and were in business with a summer job. I had accumulated $3400 and Don was able to add $3000. Which was enough to pay for the materials. The labor had to come from the two of us and this time we worked those same long hour days for the entire summer and received no hourly wage at all.

Constructing that duplex was a labor-intensive project from the ground up. We built foundation forms, mixed concrete by hand, framed up the walls, shingled the siding and the roof, sheet rocked the walls and ceilings, installed hardwood floors and windows, roughed the plumbing and the wiring, and painted everything in sight. We even built a carport. However, we were obliged to ask Pop for help with the trim, the finished plumbing and wiring, and hanging of the doors.

(Don)

We became famous in our town as the two kids, building a house at the top of their lungs. Our guy friends came by and yelled insults but the girls got a peek at bare backs with darkening muscles on the scaffolding. We sang the songs we knew accompanied by hammering and sawing. Only in a small town could one find two college boys having a yodeling contest on the top of the roof to the tune of shingling hatchets. I won the contest without much of a yodel, because my brother couldn't yodel at all. The songs quieted down and the yodeling ended when one of the neighbors complained to our mom.

We finished the duplex by the end of the summer but we discovered that our jobs had not produced the funds needed for college. Our brown tans rivaled those of the beach boys, but ours went to the waist. My brother acquired and honed his building skills quite well, but at the end of the summer, I still couldn't figure out how to use that damn square to cut a rafter angle. Our savings were gone and although each half of the duplex yielded fifty-five dollars rent, the income did not cover our school expenses. At least that summer we had accumulated an asset. Unfortunately, the cash flow from our house was smaller than we expected.

(Bob)

We returned to our respective school year jobs in Berkeley and Oakland. Don ate well as a hasher at the Tri-Delta Sorority House and we both worked for the Oakland Recreation Department. As there was no college loan program at the time, we made it through by pinching our pennies and skimping on dates. On April 15, 1963 we sold the duplex to Parden Cave from Vallejo for the sum of $13,000. Don and I each realized half of the proceeds. Don's half went mostly toward paying off a loan of $5200 that he and Shirley had borrowed from Charles Gagliardo in 1960 to purchase a house in Corcoran. The interest rate on that loan was 6%. In the summer of 1950 we learned the practical lessons of building a house, but we failed to learn the larger lesson that a property can appreciate substantially in value over time. The Duplex is still someone's home at 401 and 403 North Street in Healdsburg. It looks better than it did when it was born and it is doubtless worth well over $500,000 today.

136

The Phi-Sigs say Goodbye

The Summer of 1951
1951

(Don)

The summer of 1951 was when Bob and I learned about life on the road. I was twenty and Bob was twenty-two. Neither of us was the least bit interested in spending much time at our parents' home in Healdsburg. We had learned from the previous two summers that no matter how hard we worked, financially, we were as well off at the end of the summer as we were at the beginning. Although we didn't talk about it much, I think we understood that spending another three months at home with an unstable mother controlling every facet of our lives was not a pleasant prospect. We were interested in getting as much distance as possible from home. It was time for an adventure.

Bob worked for the Oakland Recreation Department until he was scheduled to go for six weeks to an ROTC training session at Camp Gordon, Georgia. I signed up for a seven-week summer caravan with the Presbyterian Church headquartered in Pennsylvania. I arranged a ride with my college roommate, Art Robson, who planned to drive back to New York. I told him I would split the cost of the gas as well as the driving. My last class was on Thursday afternoon and Art and I planned to leave early on Friday. By trading off we were going to make the trip to Philadelphia with three long days of driving. I needed to be at Beaver College near Philadelphia for the orientation session on Monday morning, June 16. I should have known better than to plan to leave on Friday the 13th.

On Thursday afternoon Art told me that he chose **not** to make the trip home. Since I didn't have enough money for bus fare all the way to Pennsylvania, I decided to hitch hike. Bright and early on Friday morning, after my fraternity brothers gathered on the front steps and bid me a fond farewell, my brother dropped me off, suitcase in hand on the freeway at the end of University Avenue. He said he would be in touch when his ROTC Camp was over. My task was to get from Berkeley to Philadelphia in three days. Later, Bob said that he felt a bit sorry for me standing alone there on the highway, but he thought I could take care of myself.

On the first night out, I began to realize how important it was to nap a few hours whenever possible. On the second night a truck driver named Arnie, who was traveling from Reno, Nevada to somewhere in Colorado stopped to give me a ride. He was a big, burly, man who looked mean. He eyed me and spoke in a gruff voice "I am not supposed to pick up hitch hikers but I will make an exception in your case since I'm way behind schedule and I need someone to keep me awake." I gulped, and climbed into the cab. Arnie drove all night and I kept pinching myself to keep awake. I learned that I could sleep sitting bolt upright with my eyes almost open and hold up my end of the conversation with a few grunts and a mumble or two. It took twelve hours and five days to make the trip.

I only missed two days of the orientation, but I needed sleep badly. The next day after T-Bone, the minister in charge of the Caravan program, shook me awake, he informed me that I had been teamed with two of the older students, Martha Kritzer from Pennsylvania and Carol Wirt from Baltimore, Maryland. The focus of the training period was for the teams to become bonded as a unit and since I was late, our team had to get on with the "bonding." We spent almost all our time in the team for the next three days, going to classes, eating, singing, and talking. By the end of the week we knew each other well. Martha was the team leader and Carol and I called her "Ma" because she took her responsibilities seriously and she reminded me of my mother. Martha had a hard time trying to keep Carol and me in line. The other teams had four persons assigned to them, but T-Bone implied that since we appeared to be more mature, we had only three people on ours. The truth was because of a last minute cancellation they were one caravaner short.

Our Team: Martha Kritzer, Carol Wirt, & Don Kirkpatrick

Following the orientation, the Caravan schedule called for five weeks in the field with assignments at different churches. This was to be followed by a wrap-up session back at Beaver College. Three of our one-week assignments were at small rural churches. I was surprised to discover there were small communities in New York and New Jersey. We spent two weeks at the Thirteenth Avenue Presbyterian Church in Newark, New Jersey. This was a large, all black church located in the poorer section of the city. Reverend John Dillingham, the minister, was an outgoing, warm, passionate man, and his wife; Bella knew the meaning of true hospitality. We were submerged in the black world and made to feel at home at home in a culture, significantly different from ours. Bella's laughter rang through the house at all hours, and Reverend Dillingham called to her from wherever he happened to be.

We arrived there on Saturday, June 23, and went to work teaching classes the next morning. There were sixty people listed in the church bulletin that day and twenty-five organizations. In the next two weeks it seemed we met all those people and attended most meetings of the organizations. We met with the youth fellowship, helped with the nursery, assisted with ushering, passed offering plates, and sang in the Inspirational Chorus. Our main responsibility was to organize and conduct a two-week Vacation Bible School. As soon as the three of us moved to the third floor of the manse, we were completely enveloped in the life of that church. We took our turn saying grace at meals and doing the dishes. No matter what was served, the dinner table always had room for two or three extra guests. We three white kids learned quickly how a church can impact and influence the culture of the inner city. The entire black community made Sunday its day and the church its home. It rocked with gospel music and laughter.

Bob's ROTC training was completed a few days before the wrap up session finished at Beaver College. He drove back to Georgia with his friends, Remo and Errol, in Remo's 1946 Oldsmobile. Remo planned to visit his mother in Georgia for a couple of days and then he, Errol, and Bob would pick me up in Philadelphia. The four of us planned to split the gas on the trip back to California. Then, ... Remo's mom, Myrna, decided she wanted to go to California with him.

Remo and crew picked me up in Philadelphia and the car was crammed with five passengers with luggage jammed everywhere. The car looked as if it were carrying refugees from the Oklahoma dust bowl of the 1930s. The group headed to New York City for some sight seeing before going west, and we located a cheap hotel. Remo and Myra stayed in one room and Bob, Errol, and I shared another. The walls did nothing that night to soften Myra's resentment at having to share a trip across the country with strangers. We cut short our plans to see the Rockettes and headed home with Myra scrunched petulantly in her corner of the back seat. She didn't say much but her sullenness gripped the car in an icy silence like the interior of a frozen food locker. When we stopped for gas and were seemingly out of earshot, we could hear Myra ragging on Remo. Errol was a science nut, and lobbied successfully for us to make a side trip to Washington DC to visit the Smithsonian Museum. When we finally found a parking place three blocks from the main museum building and were ready to go, Myra announced that she would wait for us in the car.

As the trip progressed the haranguing became less subtle and Myra bitched openly every chance she got. Finally, somewhere in Illinois, Bob, Errol, and I could stand it no longer and, when we next stopped for gas, Bob whispered: " That woman is just like our mom. Let's head out on our own."

Errol and I agreed and we went to the edge of the road and stuck out our thumbs. We soon found that no one picks up three hitchhikers and few will pick up two. Errol went his way and Bob and I became a twosome. We tried everything we could think of to get rides and found it difficult not to take rejection personally. We took turns sitting on each other's shoulders and made signs that said, "We tell jokes." and "We fix flats." An eight-hour wait by the side of the road in Kansas was our record. We were on the road again, and this time our task was to get close enough to California for our combined money to buy two bus tickets. Unfortunately, hunger has a way of setting its own agenda, and we found that every time we ate something or stayed in a cheap motel, it meant more hitchhiking through another state.

We finally got a ride to Denver, where we stopped to see our uncle Ray and his wife, Toot. Ray had recently suffered a stroke and was on his deathbed. Under the circumstances Toot was most gracious to Newt's two boys from California. We showered and caught up on a great deal of lost sleep. Two days later, Toot dropped us off on the outskirts of Denver where we were again at the mercy of our thumbs. Almost the first person that came by was a Colorado Highway Patrol Officer who informed us in no uncertain terms that it was against the law to hitchhike in Colorado. We told him our story and asked him what we should do.

He growled: "Well, I guess that's your problem, isn't it?" It started to rain and a kindhearted lady who was sitting on the porch listening to our conversation with the officer, called out to us when the officer left: "Hey kids, come on up here and rest your weary bones until the shower is over." We left our suitcases by the side of the road and enjoyed a cup of tea with Etta.

Later back on the road, a man in a red Oldsmobile stopped and hollered, "Hey I am headed to Reno, you fellers need a ride?" Our joy at being rescued was dampened somewhat, when we discovered the conditions. One of us would need to help Albert drive. When Bob moved into the driver's seat, Albert opened the glove compartment and pulled out the largest six-shooter I have ever seen and set it on his lap. He gestured with his gun, "I like to shoot rabbits out in the desert." That was one big conversation stopper and I think both Bob and I felt a bit like rabbits being led to the slaughter.

Albert left us off at the Greyhound bus station in Reno. Our resources finally matched the cost of two tickets to Berkeley. When we arrived back at the fraternity house, we slammed our open palms on the front door, and swore that we would never hitch hike again.

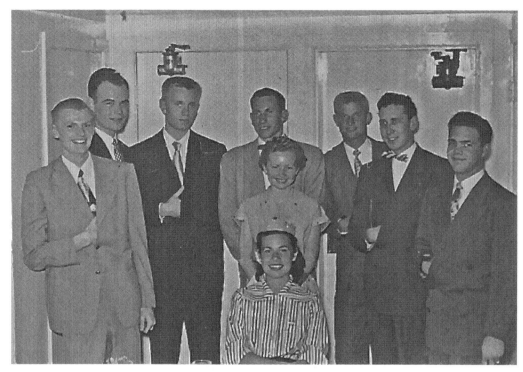

The Hashers Crown a Tri-Delt Queen

The Sling Shot
1950-52

(Don)

There had been a long history of water ballooning at the at the Phi Sig house. The following excerpt is taken from Nimitz by Elmer Belmont Potter, written in 1976: "Onnie P Lattu a young Finn, who through an oversight had been allowed to join the Naval ROTC (in 1926) before he got his American Citizenship papers became a great favorite of the Nimitz family. On one occasion he invited both Nimitz and Gunther (Lt. Commander Ernest Gunther was Nimitz's assistant.) to his fraternity house. The two officers resplendent in white uniforms, arrived in Gunther's new roadster. At that moment the fraternity brothers were engaged in tossing bags of water at each other. One such bag was aimed at Lattu who dodged and the bag hit Commander Nimitz squarely in the chest. To the amazement of all, Nimitz said nothing. He neither changed his stride nor altered his pace. He walked into the fraternity house, talked amiably with his hosts and still drippy wet, sat down to lunch, which he appeared to enjoy."

Although our mother had attended Humboldt State Teacher's College, her younger brother, Onnie, was the only member of my mother's family to attend a major university. He had received financial help from C.R. Johnson, owner of the Union Lumber Company, because he saw that Onnie was a talented young man. Uncle Onnie made the best of that opportunity and when he graduated in 1930, he ranked fourth in the NROTC program. As a result he was offered a commission in the regular navy.

(Bob)

Over the years Onnie, on his way to various naval postings would make the trip to his family home in Fort Bragg. On these trips he would always stop in Healdsburg to see his older sister, Ilma and her family. Don and I were delighted to see him because he always brought interesting things. In 1933 when he was a young ensign only two years out of UC Berkeley, he appeared on our doorstep and I remember I was disappointed he was not wearing a uniform but he did bring Don and me "teddy bears." We loved those animals dearly and I think we both still have them on our shelves.

When Don and I were in high school, Uncle Onnie offered to take us to visit the UC Berkeley Campus, where he had gone to school. We jumped at the chance. In those days school districts did not make an effort to introduce students to colleges or universities. I was a junior and Don was in the eighth grade. It was to be the only post high school campus either of us were to visit prior to actually applying for admission and there was never any question where we would go. After graduating from high school I served two years in the navy and then one year at Santa Rosa Jr. College to beef up my grades. Thus, we were both ready to head for UC Berkeley at the same time. I started as a second year transfer student but Don's grades were good enough for him to be accepted as a freshman.

(Don)

I was excited to not only be accepted into U.C. but to have my application to Bowles Hall approved as well. The Hall was a castle like building nestled in the side of the hill not far from the stadium. There were 206 young men in Bowles that year and many were leaders in various activities as well as in the political life of the campus. Even then, it was obvious that these boys would be leaders in the larger world one day. At Healdsburg High School, I lettered on the varsity football, and track teams and participated in everything from band to Dramatics Club. My grade point average was near the top of the class and I left home feeling I was ready for what life would offer. However, I found entering U.C. as a freshman was a daunting experience. I was too small to make the football team, there were others who had faster times in the sprints, and I could not play trumpet well enough to make the Marching Band. I did join the Cal Glee Club and the Rally Committee. My folks paid for my room and board for my freshman year but when I turned nineteen in May of 1950, I needed to be independent and said to my dad, "Pop, from now on I will pay for my own room and board. You can save your money for Betty's education."

(Bob)

I joined the Phi Sigma Kappa Fraternity House as a result of Onnie's introduction and encouragement. The G.I. Bill rewarded my two-year stint in the navy with a monthly stipend and while it wasn't much, it paid for my House food bill. I didn't have to find a hashing job, which provided me with study time.

(Don)

Since Bob and I exhausted our savings in building the duplex during the summer, I discovered the reality of my newly established independence. I could no longer afford to live at Bowles Hall and I didn't have a GI Bill stipend to help me out. My brother and a couple of good Healdsburg friends put the muscle on me at the right time. They argued I could live cheaper at "the House" with twenty-five other guys in the sleeping porch. I caved in and joined the Fraternity.

I found out the University was not like high school. It was difficult to work thirty hours a week at the Oakland Recreation Department, hash at the Tri-Delt House for meals, keep up with Rally Committee and Cal Glee Club activities, and still carry a full academic load. In addition I now had parties to attend and girls to date. Something had to give. My grades tanked and I found myself on "academic probation." I minimized activities, concentrated on enjoying fraternity life, doing my homework and earning enough to support myself, but I couldn't let the girls go.

Don Kirkpatrick, John Miksits, Cookie, & Mitch Jasinski

(Bob)

When our uncle was in the fraternity, it was called Sigma Phi Sigma but it became Phi Sigma Kappa sometime in the 1930s. The fraternity house was located on Warring Street two doors down from the Tri Delt House and a half block from the south side of the stadium. As long as anyone can remember, water ballooning during finals week had been an honored custom. Students would finish their exams and "let off steam" by rushing home to carry boxes of water balloons to the third story roof. Those students who dallied on exam day would have to dodge a barrage of balloons or miss supper. Some times the girls from the Delta Gamma Sorority on the next street up the hill would meet the guys in the vacant lot between the streets and engage in a playful war of balloons. While the guys could throw harder, the girls had the advantage of being able to throw down hill.

144

(Don)

One day Bob gathered some friends together and said. "Let's build a water balloon catapult." The war of water was about to be equalized. The crew constructed a wooden frame, which resembled a gigantic slingshot. They affixed heavy strips of rubber cut from a truck inner tube, attached a large leather pouch at its end and called the apparatus "Alice." Those doubters in the group had to "eat their words" because it worked beyond expectations. With Bob holding down the frame, Rob Pierce and Dick Gardella pulled the sling back as far as they could and let the balloon fly. The first water missile splattered on the street in front of the sorority house.

Bob said: " I think we need more lift and a bit more thrust. I'll see if any more of the guys are around." He came back to the roof with Mitch Jasinski and Pete Goodwagen. With Bob aiming, the four guys stretched Alice's bands tight and let the balloon fly. The second shot silenced the group in the front yard as like a rainbow the balloon arched for a full city block before punching a neat hole in a third story window of the Delta Gamma House.

Dick said: "Oh, that was a fluke. Let's try it again." and the third try shattered a downstairs plate glass window.

" Oh, Oh, Bob exclaimed, "This is getting expensive. We'd better quit."

(Bob)

The broken Delta Gamma windows were more than we bargained for. Nevertheless, after a truce was called, the House President offered apologies, and a crew cleaned up the glass damage, a notice was put on the bulletin board asking for volunteers to replace the windows. By dinnertime, sixteen names had appeared on the sheet. The President had to reduce the volunteers to a workable crew and drew names to see who could have the job.

(Don)

For a week the slingshot sat alone on the roof but at the dinner table the conversation always to got around to how good Alice actually was. The outcome of those conversations went something like this.

Jasinski, frustrated that there was much talk but nothing was happening said, "I will bet ten dollars that we can loft a balloon inside the stadium."

Ron Guptil replied: "You're on." and Ron, Mitch, and Br-uce Kelly went to work repositioning Alice so that she faced north instead of east.

Ron said, "Next Saturday, the football team is playing in Minnesota. Let's try it out then." Mitch replied, "I will get a couple of guys to stand outside the fence and watch. Let's schedule the shot for 1:00 sharp. Set your watch with mine"

The test did happen and once again a water balloon was lofted high in the sky and over the rim of the football stadium. Fortunately, only the grounds workers were in the stadium to witness the event but they must have been pretty excited to see those water balloons coming at them. The next day, Bob called the crew together and said, "You know, guys I think our fun is over, Hootman and Mulliner saw a campus police car cruising down the block this morning. I think we'd better dismantle Alice."

The Cal-Stanford Game (1952)

The Phi Sigma Kappa House

The Tub
1951-52

(Don)

It was rumored that one of the girls who lived in the A.E. Phi Sorority house annex next door had an interesting tattoo on her right shoulder and the conversation in the living room became hot and heavy. Half of the group was chanting "birthmark, birthmark, birthmark." The others responded "tattoo, tattoo, tattoo." I entered the room and said: " Hey, what in the world are you guys talking about ?"

Rob Pierce responded, "Dumb ass, get with it. Haven't you been up to third floor, recently?"

"No, what do you mean, anyway?"

"Go up and look."

I trudged up the stairs to see a group of guys standing by the stairway. One stood on a chair, and looked out the top of the window. When my turn came, I saw what they were talking about. The shade on the small bathroom window on the second story of the AEPhi Annex, which was normally closed was now partly open and we could see the half dressed girls as they washed. A whole new world had opened up. I joined the birthmark team because I thought a tattoo on a sophisticated AEPhi was just not possible. Besides in 1951 tattoos were rarely seen on anyone.

The shade stayed open for most of that spring. Either the girls never noticed the peepers from above, or it was left open on purpose. The relatively tame activity kept the guys occupied for several weeks until spring break put the show on hold.

My brother, Bob who was a mischief genius, had a way of getting others to help with his dirty work. The guys at the Phi Sig house did not claim to be angels, but they needed a creative person to point the way and Bob was that leader.

There were two sinks in the bathroom next door and, if one strained his neck at the very top of the window, he could almost see a shower in the back corner. One day, Rob, after his turn at the lookout station, said, "Gee it's too bad the girls don't have a bath tub in that room."

With an evil glint in his eye, Bob replied, "Wait a minute. I saw an old bathtub at the dump last week, why don't we do the girls a favor and get it for them?"

The Committee, which instantly volunteered could hardly wait for the break, because the girls were required to leave for home and the annex would be closed for a full week. On Saturday evening, Rob reporting from a scouting trip, said: "Well, guys, we are out of luck. All the windows and doors are locked tight."

With a thoughtful expression Bob pursed his lips: "What about the second story, let's get the ladder from the storage shed."

It turned out that no one had locked the upstairs bathroom window and the adventure was on. Bob had no difficulty recruiting help and it took six muscular boys to edge that bathtub through the front door and up the stairs. They turned the tub on its side, scraped it into the bathroom and positioned it in the middle of the bathroom floor. The tub was filled with concrete blocks and a three inch steel pipe extended from its middle. Bob and his crew filled the tub with sacks of redi-mixed concrete and let it set for a week.

The following Monday afternoon two campus policemen hammered at the front door. Dick Gardella, who was the best actor in the house, put on a face of innocence and opened the door. One of the officers said, "Ahummm, were any of the boys here in the house over the break?"

Dick turned and yelled, "Hey, were any of you guys around last week ?"
Responses came from different parts of the house. "Well, come on down the cops are here."
The policemen then asked the group at the door. "Did any of you notice anything unusual or suspicious going on next door?"

The well-rehearsed replies were convincingly casual and uniformly negative. "Well, if anyone remembers anything, please give me a call." and he extended his card.

Dick replied. "We certainly will let you know, officer."

As they left, Bob observed one policeman put his hand over his mouth to suppress a grin. From that point on the girls could be observed kneeling on the tub as they leaned over the basin to brush their teeth. Finally, several weeks later workers arrived next door and the sound of a jack hammer could be heard resonating throughout the neighborhood. It was rumored around the house that they had to knock a hole in the wall to remove the offending tub.

Addendum:

The incident made the San Jose Mercury News, but the police never found the miscreants. Rob Pierce, who majored in chemistry, established his own chemical company. When he sold it, he enjoyed life as a multi millionaire. Rich Gardella was a successful attorney in Santa Clara County. Bob Kirkpatrick was a superintendent of schools for some thirty-five years. He retired as Mendocino County Superintendent of Schools in 1989.

The Hashers Crown Kathy Benson

The Tri-Delts Get Even
1951-52

(Don)

It was the fall of 1951 and I was still discovering what life was all about. I was one of seven hashers who served dinner and did the dishes for the Delta Delta Delta Sorority house at U.C. Berkeley. Art Robson and I were known as houseboys and were allowed to live in a room in the basement. We were expected to do the grunt work around the house and we were the envy of all who knew us, because how many college boys could say that they lived in a sorority house?

149

At the end of an evening of study, when the housemother wasn't around, we occasionally joined the girls in the kitchen for an evening snack. As a result of our proximity we got to know some of the Tri-Delts well and they, us. The hashers were a good-humored group and we thought of ways to tease the girls. We served a second dessert to someone who flunked a midterm, or deliberately skipped a girl who was engrossed in heavy conversation. Each semester we selected one girl to be *Hasher Queen,* which meant she had to help scrub pots that night. However, we soon realized the girls were pretty good at teasing as well.

The house had three floors and Art and I assisted girls moving in and out. We carried large boxes and suitcases upstairs on occasion, but were always accompanied by the floor manager, who preceded us and announced in a loud voice. "Man on first floor" Then when we climbed the next flight of stairs: "Man on second floor" Presumably, those announcements would alert any partially clothed females to cover up and close doors.

One day when the housemother was shopping, Art and I were asked to move a large trunk upstairs. It was heavy and required us to use both arms. We passed the first floor without mishap, but when we got to the second floor, we had to hoist the trunk to the other set of stairs. Halfway down the hall, the announcement, "Man on second floor" triggered an unexpected event. All the doors opened at the same time and scantily clad girls scurried from one room to another. Both Art and I tried to cover our eyes with one hand, but the trunk *thumped* to the floor, and with mouths open, we stood there until the doors closed again. The girls had evened the score.

Sunning in the Tri-Delt Backyard

Brown Street House

1954 - 64

Step on a Crack
1946-1958
(Betty)

School Days

"Step on a crack, break your mother's back" – Carefully I would recite this little poem over and over as I walked the four blocks to school each morning from our house on North Street. Often I would stop and pick chickweed for Dicky bird while I passed by the houses I had memorized. The Grammar School was on the corner near our house.

I went to the first grade with Miss Schwab just as my brothers had gone before. However, I began in the middle of the year, because I had been attending Grant School with my mother. On the first day, the class was busy writing the names of two presidents: George Washington, and Abraham Lincoln. Each child held the over sized pencil and carefully traced the letters of the names. If the spelling was correct, Miss Schwab promised a reward of a stamped picture of Lincoln on our papers. I sat down in the back row and wrote, but I wasn't certain how to spell those long complicated names. The reward was important to me so I remember peeking at Gail Grove's paper to see how to spell "Abraham." I wanted a picture too. When she stamped my paper, I felt uneasy because I hadn't earned the reward legitimately.

I was talkative and got in trouble because I found it hard to stay quiet. Each day she shushed me over and over. When I got home in the afternoons, I talked excitedly about the day and everything that happened, but my mother shushed me as well. One day I said in exasperation "If I have to be quiet at school, and quiet at home, when am I going to learn to talk?"

I settled down and in the second grade, found myself bored because I finished the work before the other children. The teacher suggested I write a story. That idea appealed to me so I wrote about my trip to Mars. I solicited pictures from other students who contributed pictures of Martians, space ships, and monsters. I wrote the story and created my first "novel."

In 1951 our town adopted a battalion in Korea. We were asked to bring soap, washcloths, and toothbrushes to school so we could send them overseas to the soldiers. We wrote letters and I received one or two in return from soldiers in Korea. At the end of the War, the battalion sent money and built the playground equipment on the Grammar school playground. A movie was made of the process of gathering and sorting the food and other items. I stood in line in the hall as the bright lights of the camera panned over us recording this important moment in history.

Plays interested me and in the third grade, I found one in Mom's teacher magazine about discovering gold at the end of the rainbow, and staged it in the cafeteria. Another time I wrote a modern "hip" version of Little Red Riding Hood, which I organized for a school assembly. One of my favorite movies was *Helzapoppin,* a zany comedy of people passing through the movie set at odd moments. I sometimes arranged the routines in the middle of assemblies.

(Guy walks in with a briefcase "Where are you going?"

"I'm going to court." He exits.

Same guy enters ten minutes later with a ladder.) He is asked again, "Where are you going this time?"

"I'm going to a higher court.")

At one assembly I ran through the audience several times looking and calling for Arnie. Finally I found him – he was a flea behind Gail Grove's ear.

When I was in the sixth grade the school was crowded. Classes were held in all the available spaces including the cafeteria, where we had class together with the fifth grade. The auditorium held several classes simultaneously. That year an annex was constructed along the side of the building. The seventh and eighth grades were the first classes to occupy the new building.

1954

In the eighth grade, I got the idea we should have a "crazy day" when everyone dressed up in funny clothes and came to school. My brothers had talked about a dress up day in High School, and I thought we should do the same. When I proposed it to Mr. Gibbs, our principal, he liked the idea. As a result we all dressed up and came to school in costume. It was a great deal of fun.

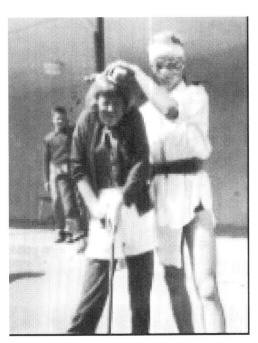

Larry Morgan and Betty on Eighth Grade Dress Up Day

We experienced our first graduation when we finished the eighth grade, and I was chosen to speak at the commencement ceremony as valedictorian. Our science teacher, Mr. Manley was a wonderful cartoonist, a fact he kept well hidden. When I saw one of his drawings, I was enthralled. I pestered him to draw one for me because I adored his art. On the day of the commencement, he presented me with a pencil sketch of my address at the commencement, entitled "Onward", the theme of our graduation. He entitled it "Betty Boop." Holding the picture in my hands, I felt on top of the world. His gift has stayed in my memory all my life. The picture still hangs over my desk.

153

Mr. Manley's Drawing of Betty Boop

1955

Our class was the first to make the transition from an eight grade Grammar school - four grade High School, to a Grammar, Junior High, High School system. For one year we occupied the large white school on Grant Street. I loved Junior High and the principal, Mr. Malone. We had elections for student body officers and I ran for president. Aided with advice from my brothers, I began my campaign. I made colorful badges saying "Kirky for president", and put a large sign on the school fence saying "Don't be on the fence, vote for Betty", but I never made much headway with the voters, until one day when I staged an event in the hallway at lunchtime. Bill Jacobson and Tucker Zimmerman argued and fought in loud voices, which immediately aroused the attention of everyone in the hall. Bill demanded that Tucker vote for me, but Tucker refused, as he yelled and ran down the hall. Bill pulled out a large realistic cap gun and shot him with a loud bang. Staging a spectacular death, Tucker fell. Anne Zobel strode over to Tucker and planted a tombstone on his chest saying, "Here lies Freddy, He didn't vote for Betty." Tucker lay in the hallway for a good twenty minutes while everyone walked around him commenting on the scene they had just witnessed. I won the election.

Pete Peterson and I used to pantomime to Spike Jones records for assemblies. One stood out: Liberace played the piano while his brother George, sang "I'm in the Mood for Love". We rehearsed it after school for days until we had it down pat. It was popular with the kids in the audience. When we graduated, I was the valedictorian speaker.

In high school I was particularly anxious to make good grades and I asked my brother Bob how to make an A in class. By then he was teaching himself, and I respected what he thought. He said, "Always read the chapter ahead of the one you are working on, and do more than is expected of you." That advice stuck with me, especially that year when I was struggling in Geometry. Everyone knew Norman Ray was the mathematical genius in our class, but I wanted to beat him in math. Every night when we had homework, I diligently read the next chapter in the book ahead of where we were. When Miss Luce asked a question at the end of the class it usually involved the necessity of knowing material in the new chapter. I raised my hand with the answer and she thought I was smart. Norman knew the answer as well but he didn't have to read the chapter. The day we were assigned the Pythagorean theorem, I took it home and worked for hours until I solved it. To my surprise, I was the first in the class to get it, although Norman was second and I was once again Valedictorian speaker. The commencement experiences prepared me for being on the graduation platform at American University where I led the National Anthem for more than thirty years.

A Beautiful New Home
1954

(Betty)

While we were staying in the duplex on North Street, Pop was building a home on Brown Street. It was beautiful. The walkway was paved with used-brick, and I recall seeing Pop kneeling in the sand, laying each brick carefully one by one. In the middle of the breezeway between the garage and the main house was a loose brick with a recessed space beneath where we kept the key to the front door. The living room was sunny with large windows, which looked out on the lot, high off the corner of Powell and Brown Streets. There was a retaining wall of used brick, which shored up the hill. We had a lovely lawn and a patio in the back, where I sunbathed. I slept in the master bedroom with a sliding glass door onto the patio. Pop built a room off the garage where he slept.

When the house was being built, mother knew that she would have the bedroom at the head of the hall. She complained that she did not like the location of the closet and harangued Dad to move it, but he refused. When he was gone for a few days, she hired the husband of one of her Finnish friends to remove it and lay in the framework of a second closet where she wanted, near the entrance to the room. After it was changed, she realized she didn't like it after all. When Pop returned, he hit the roof. He complained that she had hired a "jackleg" carpenter to do the job, and it was not up to his standards. Meekly, she asked him to move the closet back where it was before, which he did. I didn't hear any more complaining about the layout of the rooms after that.

Mom went to great care to decorate the house and consulted a designer in Santa Rosa to arrange the decor. The carpet was a wall-to-wall rose-colored rug, which matched the stone in the fireplace. Ancient gold Tibetan figures postured and gamboled on an aqua colored background across the expanse of the dining room wall. The sofa curved around the corner of the living room, and matched the colors of the fireplace as well. The table in the kitchen was wrought iron, and the stove

156

was electric. It folded up against the wall to allow for counter space. Even the dishes were new – the latest style of the time, in chartreuse, gray and aqua. The curtains were custom made – not like the ready-made ones on North Street or the bare windows in the mountain house. They were cream colored and ran from floor to ceiling and wall-to-wall. When they were installed, they had to be tied back in pleats for several days to ensure they hung perfectly. Mom enjoyed the house and had few fits as we moved in.

Testing the Waters

(Betty)

When I was in high school I asked my brother Don if he had ever left home. He mentioned that he had one time, but it hadn't been very successful. I made up my mind I was not going to bear the intolerable rages any longer, and the next time Mom had a temper tantrum I would inform her either she stop or I would leave. This was a huge step in asserting who I was, and I wasn't certain I had the courage to do it.

The next morning she was in a raging fit about what I was wearing to school, and she began throwing my clothes all over the room and tearing them in pieces. I warned her that if she didn't stop, I wasn't going to come home that evening. She persisted, so I decided to follow my morning declaration.

I went to Gail Grove's home, two blocks away. I let my father know where I was and called home to inform my mother I wasn't coming home until she apologized. She snapped that I could stay where I was forever, for she had no intention of apologizing to me.

The next day after school I sneaked home to get some clothes, a comb, and a toothbrush. When I let myself in the house, I was shocked to find every bit of evidence I had been a part of the family was gone. All clothes, pictures, piano music, and school papers were gone. My closets were cleaned out and all drawers were empty. There were no pictures of me on the wall. I had no piano music. I had been erased.

She discovered where I was staying, and called to demand I return home because I was causing an expense for the Groves. In her clipped and angry voice she said this was inexcusable and selfish on my part. When I again asked her to apologize, she refused and hung up on me. By then I hadn't been home for five or six days. When my father called and said I should return because it was the best thing to do, I realized things were pretty hairy for him at home because of me. I returned home although my mother never apologized. I wish I could say standing up to her temper made things better, but it did not. Things were much worse afterward, I did find out what happened to my belongings. She had put them in the trunk of her car.

Pom-Poms

(Betty)

During my high school years, I lived on Brown Street, and walked to school every morning. I was a pom-pom girl with five of my friends. We practiced routines and shook pom-poms jumping up and down at the football and basketball games. My black-skirted corduroy jumper fell to mid-calf, and stood out with full petticoats. It looked great when we cheered. We wore a white sweater underneath, which had a big red H on the front.

One day when we were boarding the school bus to go to Cloverdale, I realized I left my red and black pom-poms home. The girls were upset because if I were the only one without pom-poms, our routine would be spoiled. I ran back into the building and called my father from the principal's office. I described what I needed and stressed that the pom-poms were essential and he needed to hurry because we were getting ready to leave on the bus. I was desperate.
He agreed to find them and rush over. We were all seated on the bus when my Dad's blue Chevy truck turned the corner and came down the long drive to the school. Everyone cheered as we saw him coming and I raced to the front of the bus to get my pom-poms. What he handed me was a pair of castanets. Mortified, I made my way to the back of the bus with every eye on me. The kids taunted and teased me. A decision was made. The five of us made-do with only one pom-pom in our right hands. It must have worked, because our team won.

Mom & Betty

158

Betty's World of Work

Impressing the Folks
1956

(Betty)

When I was at the University of the Pacific and engaged to Curtis Casey, I traveled several times to Sacramento to visit Casey's parents. They were large people, and basic in their fundamental religious beliefs. Their philosophy was simple: go to church every Sunday, no swearing, no drinking, no movies, no card playing, and sing hymns at home for entertainment. They were nice, but stern. I was surprised when I heard it had been more than twenty years since they had been to the theater or to a movie. There were good movies available and many of them were inspirational and carried a message. I convinced Curtis we should take his parents to the movies to show them what the world was like and it wasn't so bad. "After all," I said, "They could be inspired by the beauty of a great film. There is beautiful scenery, good acting, a lovely message which could reinforce their belief in God."

Curtis worked on his parents, and eventually, they relented. They agreed to share this wonderful experience. Curtis researched the movies, asked for good suggestions from his brothers at the fraternity who were familiar with the recent films and came up with one befitting the occasion. It was entitled *"The Immortal Mr. T"*. He scoured the local paper and found a theater nearby their house where the film was playing. On the day of the event I could hardly contain my excitement. We were doing something for them they would enjoy. As I was getting out of the car with his parents, Curtis ran ahead and secured the tickets. We just had to go into the theater. We were a few minutes early, but another film had begun. We made our way to our seats in the dark, carefully stepping by the other people in the row to sit in the center for a good view. I was wedged in between Curtis' mother and father - Curtis was sitting to his mother's right.

I didn't pay attention to the screen until we were comfortably seated, and was astounded to look up and observe a rather grainy black and white film with a nude woman sunning herself on a high precipice. She dove into a pool, with the announcer extolling the beauty of her various endowments. I had never seen a nude body in films before and was in a state of shock. His father blanched and stiffened in his seat next to me.

"What is this Curtis?" he hissed, leaning across me and grabbing him by the sleeve.
"I don't know. This isn't supposed to be the film." he whispered back, "The one we came for has beautiful color and acting."

His father settled back into his seat, reluctantly. We endured the first film, which was mercifully short. The Caseys squirmed uncomfortably in their seats and I averted my eyes and held my breath anxiously. Finally the film ended, and the screen switched to glorious color. I relaxed, taking a deep breath.

"Finally" I thought, "we can see what we came for."
As the film unfolded, it became painfully clear this was not what we had in mind for his parents. The film was about a man who had x-ray eyes and could see through the clothes of any woman he met and he met many - all of them were well endowed.

160

"OK, we're going" his father exclaimed reaching over me and pulling his wife to her feet. We exited quickly through the dark rows, stumbling over the feet of other patrons, not even stopping to mumble an apology. As we emerged into the sunlight, they raced to the car, but I was overcome by curiosity. What was that film? How could Curtis have been so far off? I peered up at the marquee. There in red letters was the answer to the puzzle. Blinking down at me were the words: *"The Immoral Mr. Tease."*

Addendum:

Mom was usually on good behavior when we brought people home. When I announced I wanted the family to meet the parents of my fiancé, she had a plan. We always ate at home, having a family dinner to meet people and converse around the dinner table. That was our family custom. This time, Mom absolutely refused to cook, so my father and I suggested we take them out to dinner. She decided that we would go to the Flamingo Hotel in Santa Rosa, fourteen miles away. When I began to climb into the car to be with my fiancé, Mom yanked me out and insisted we ride separately I would ride with her, and Curtis, with his parents. I was suspicious about this plan, for I could see the familiar pattern of behavior surfacing. When we got into the car, she floor-boarded the car, whipping around corners, making switchbacks and going down alleys trying to lose the other car. She couldn't lose them and was hopping mad when they drove up in front of the Flamingo hotel. I could see how furious Curtis' Dad was. Mom had made her point - I had a mother who was "over the top" and therefore, unsuitable for marriage. Curtis broke up with me a short few months later. The reason? Who knows?

Curtis Casey and Elizabeth Many Years Later

Away at College
1958-1962

(Betty)
Pacific Music Camp

In 1958 I headed to the College of the Pacific. I chose it because it was where my friends were going. Ironically, I didn't see them more than one or two times the four years I was there. Three months before I entered, I went to a three-week music camp COP offered. This was my first exposure to other people my age who were seriously interested in music. I fell in love with singing and music that summer.

I had a crush on our chorus conductor, Lynn Scholand, a young teacher from Ashland. One day, he asked me to go with him to the Fourth of July fireworks celebration. I was exited at being asked out by someone I admired. It turned out to be a double date with Taso Vrenios and the star singer of the workshop, Mickey. That evening I learned both Taso and Lynn were enamored with Mickey.

While at camp, I was exposed to my first opera *The Devil and Daniel Webster*. Although I was fourth understudy for the lead, and the second chorus girl in the back row, I loved singing in a stage production - especially an opera. Taso was the lead: Daniel Webster. He had a magnificent voice for a high school senior – full and robust. We became great friends in camp and continued that friendship during college.

Paul Switzler and Betty Kirkpatrick at Pacific Music Camp

I received a scholarship for my first year as an English major. After the incredible musical experience of the Pacific Music camp, it didn't take long to realize I wanted to enter the conservatory as a music major. In the middle of the semester I went to the office in the conservatory and asked to be admitted as a piano major. With great anticipation the conservatory doors opened and I knew it was what I wanted to do with the rest of my life. I was dismayed to discover every other pianist there played circles around me. Since I was studying voice as part of the curriculum, I asked my voice teacher, Elizabeth Spelts, if I could be a voice major. Her reply "As well as anybody" was all I needed. Studying voice was exactly right for me. It was what I wanted to do all along. I blossomed and spent as much time in the practice room as I could. This was a far cry from being forced to practice the piano with mother wielding a yardstick. Mom insisted I get an education degree as well as a music degree so I needed to be a double major, and take more courses.

Zeta Phi

While at Pacific, I joined the sorority, Zeta Phi where most of the music majors lived. It went national in 1961 and became Alpha Chi Omega. When I was a senior I received the national honor scholarship as "outstanding senior Alpha Chi in the United States." I suspected my voice teacher had submitted my name.

163

I went with a young man, Curtis Casey. As he was a fraternity boy, we were "pinned" and eventually engaged. The pinning night was memorable. I was studying in my room, barefoot with hair rolled up, and wearing pajamas. My sorority sisters heard singing outside the front door and someone rushed into our room saying we had to come down to the front porch. We tumbled down the stairs, still in PJs. Curtis' entire fraternity was outside our house in a semicircle singing. They hustled me to the front and Curtis presented me with his fraternity pin.

In my senior year I went home for semester break. Mother was in an agitated state when I arrived and a major fight occurred. Without a word she grabbed her car keys and stalked out of the house. Pop wasn't home either and I didn't know why. This was pre planned for she had packed a suitcase beforehand. I was afraid to leave the house for fear she would have a screaming fit if she came home and found me gone. That house felt like a prison for a week. She wanted to punish me, because she didn't come back until the day before I was scheduled to return to college. She walked into the house as if nothing happened. There was no apology or explanation.

Imitating my brothers

I made good friends at the university and many lived with me in the sorority. Ginger Tucker was a junior when I was a freshman and I admired her spunk and drive. She organized a madrigal group and we performed all over Stockton. It was there I learned about madrigals, how to read, sing in tune, and be an ensemble member. We met three times every week to practice. We were devoted to Ginger and the group. We sat around a table in performance as the old madrigal singers did centuries before.

Ginger's Madrigal Group

I teased Ginger and played tricks on her. She responded with her own. One day my large black and white stuffed whale mascot, Wally, was missing from my bed. It was unmistakable as it was almost as big as me. He had been stolen and I was devastated. Later that day at our conservatory class we saw him hanging from the second story window in front of the building. I was slow to retrieve him and for several days, Wally was upside down in full view of everyone who entered and left the conservatory. Years later Ginger sent me a song she wrote about Wally. She had been using it in her music classes in Los Angeles.

"Wally The Whale" Getting Fresh Air

Our a cappella choir met three times a week under Mr. Russell Bodley and we considered it a source of pride. We toured California and sang at the Sunrise Service in Yosemite on Easter. It was the latest one in the United States as the sun crawled over Half Dome before peeking into Mirror Lake at approximately 10:00 a.m. We stood on one side of the lake and sang anthems and songs. It was a thrill to see the lake reflecting the sky and hear our voices echoing back from the canyon. That evening we gave a concert in the Ahwahnee Lodge for the guests.

I loved playing tricks and while on tour, I sometimes put messages into the music of an unsuspecting singer. One time, when we sang the Bach double Motets, which requires incredible concentration, I taped a picture and statement from a magazine into the music of the singer standing next to me. It said "I dreamed I sang a Bach Motet in my Maiden form Bra." When my "victim" turned the page, his body stiffened. I was so delighted with my joke that I lost composure more than he did.

Learning to be an Opera Singer

My first operatic role was in *The Outcasts of Poker Flat* by Stan Beckler, a faculty member of the conservatory. It was a world premiere with orchestra conducted by Russell Bodley and directed by Marcus Brown. I had the role of Piney Woods, the young girl who dies in the woods. I was thrilled to be on stage in a live performance. As I lay in the arms of Bruce Brown, the tenor, I reached up and caressed his face with little pats and caresses. I was reminded of the old movies I had seen and was trying to recreate the feelings of the movie stars. The director stopped me with a shout "Miss Kirkpatrick, what in the world are you doing?"

I said, "I am trying to act as if I am dying".

"For heavens sake, we are on the stage, not on the movie screen. JUST LIE STILL!"

At that moment I realized acting on the stage and in movies was very different.

*

At Pacific I had the opportunity to be in a musical and was excited because musicals were a passion of mine. I had watched many on the screen. This one was an early musical bordering on operetta entitled *Leave it to Jane*. I had the secondary comic role with a big solo number entitled "Poor Prune." I could relate to that as our family lived on a prune ranch.

*

The conservatory put on an opera every year under the direction of Dr. Lucas Underwood. He was a dynamic man, who conducted the orchestra, and organized the staging, costumes, sets and lighting as well. He was a one-man show. I wanted to be in the larger operatic production but the choice roles were given to upper class men In my junior year Faust was the production, and I worked hard the previous summer to sing the aria of Siebel, the page, for auditions. When Dr. Underwood was ready to select the soloists, he didn't have auditions, but announced that he would cast Siebel as a tenor rather than a soprano and he was going to cast Taso. The second cast was a young soprano, who was a beauty queen. When I asked Dr. Underwood why he didn't listen to my prepared audition, he told me I didn't look like a boy in pants, but neither did Miss "Beauty Queen."

In our senior year the opera Masked Ball was chosen and I was cast in the leading role of Amelia. Taso was cast in the tenor role, Ricardo. What a thrill it was to perform Verdi's soaring music. We sang our hearts out. Singing opposite Taso in the opera was exciting as we were enamored with each other. In the final performance after the second act duet, the tenor and soprano sing passionately and then embrace. That night we wailed! We came to the embrace and held it until the audience stopped clapping. The applause wouldn't stop and we held the embrace for more than two minutes. During that time Taso whispered in my ear for the first time "I love you." This was one of the high points in my musical performances. I no longer felt engaged to Curtis. Afterward, mother commented caustically that the embrace went on a little too long. Little did she know!

Mrs. Dakserhof came to the performance that night, took me aside and said, "You see, you have 'IT.' That is rare." I had never been complemented on my performances in such a way. It stayed with me for many years.

I reached my 21st birthday during the time we were working on the opera, and as I had never imbibed before, the cast took me out after rehearsal for a drink. I made arrangements to stay overnight with Alice Brady, one of the sopranos I knew, and we went to a bar in the neighborhood. Each cast member treated me to a favorite drink and it was a large cast. I learned there are many different drinks and I drank one of everything: daiquiris, manhattans, black Russians, mai tais and more. I was totally inebriated and truly sick. At the end of the evening the entire group stuffed itself into the car and drove circles around the sorority after curfew, singing "Happy Birthday, Betty" at the top of their lungs. I was so sick I was in bed for two days. The word got around because I was teased royally when I returned to classes.

The University Conservatory had its annual Senior Performance Night with the orchestra, and it was customary for all seniors to perform. I sang Micaela's aria from Carmen. My parents were there, arriving just before the concert. My mother was in a state of agitation, as she had not been invited to the reception held beforehand. Whether or not I deliberately forgot to inform her remains a mystery to me. I wasn't up to her shenanigans before I had to perform, and subconsciously I failed to tell her about the reception.

That evening I was singled out and recognized with a certificate for being the outstanding student of the conservatory. This was a humbling experience as many fine musicians studied there. After the concert, the lobby was filled with well-wishers from the faculty and conservatory, and there were my parents - my mother tapping her foot and twitching with her lips pressed firmly together. "Well, there you are. Why weren't we invited to the reception before? Aren't we good enough?" I was embarrassed as her strident voice cut through the crowd and heads began to turn.

"Let's go outside Mom, we can talk better there." and I led them out.

"Humph", she groused, "You were the worst one up there. I was ashamed of you."

Her tirade caught me off guard and a hard lump lodged itself in my chest and throat. I found my breathing difficult and suddenly I couldn't talk. Mother had an uncanny way of knowing exactly what to say to make her comments as hurtful as possible. I looked around for psychological and emotional help and saw Taso and his sister approaching. He saw the pain in my face and suggested we go to the car. We walked the several blocks to the car with mother sniping at me the entire way. When we got there she reached up and pulled the crystal beads, which were a gift from Taso's sister Kanella, off my neck, and broke them in the process. She shoved me against the car and tried to shove them down my throat and cut my face. Taso tugged her off and pulled me away to his car with his sister inside. The event didn't upset me as much as the fact that not one word was said about my hard-won honor as outstanding student of the graduating class. I was puzzled why my father remained in the background, saying nothing.

Summer times

During the summers I didn't want to go home and tried to find work, which forced me to stay on campus. The first summer I acted as a resident assistant in one of the dorms and took summer classes. The next summer I worked in the housing office and stayed with several sorority sisters off campus. The final summer before my senior year, I had the opportunity to go to Europe with my voice teacher, Elizabeth Spelts and her companion Shirley Turner.

It was a great opportunity to be in Europe for three months, including six weeks traveling across Italy, Switzerland and Germany. Another student, Louise Longley went along as well. Louise and I spent the first few weeks traveling with Elizabeth and Shirley crowded in a VW. Elizabeth drove most of the time, and she had a mind of her own when it came to speed and right-of-way. When we drove over the mountain from Switzerland to Italy she was angry about something and drove very fast over narrow roads, suited only for one-way traffic. Louise and I sitting in the back of the VW, wedged between suitcases closed our eyes in fear of driving off the cliff. We made it to Rome in record time, but Elizabeth in her typical American arrogance, refused to give the right of way to a rather large truck driven by an aggressive Italian. We collided and a great deal of yelling and arguing ensued with no solution. We drove away with the VW dented yet running. We stopped in Trieste and looked at the sea. While I was gazing at the ocean, an Italian soldier came up to me and asked where was I planning to sleep that night. I was nonplussed at the question. Wherever I went those several weeks, I heard wolf whistles and suggestive comments from the Italian men.

In Munich we stayed at an apartment of two spinsters, Daisy and Tony Diesel. Daisy was the sister of Rudolf Diesel who invented the Diesel engine and was an artist. She asked me what I would like her to paint, and I gave her a photo I had taken of a lake in Italy – Lago Maggiore. She painted it and gave it to me. I cherish it to this day.

After Shirley and Elizabeth left for America on a ship from Italy, Louise met her family and continued to travel with them. I met two of my sorority sisters and we traveled for another month. We had a u-rail pass and decided to go wherever we wanted. We stayed in hostels, which required us to have sheets or a sleeping bag. We had neither, but slept on bare mattresses each night. We stayed in a huge room filled with beds and young people traveling on a budget. I slept with my money belt under me each night, fearful of having my passport and money stolen. As light as I traveled, I found my big white suitcase became heavier as I hauled it down the roads to our nightly hostel.

We were in Munich for a couple of days and went to the Hofbrau Haus for beer and to experience the ambiance. The three of us sat in a huge room with long tables and I had my first beer. The friendly Germans enjoyed themselves singing and toasting everyone. We joined in the singing with a German couple sitting across from us. They took pictures of the "three young American girls in Germany for the first time" and promised to send them to us. I was skeptical, but several weeks later I received a picture of the evening from that German couple.

American Soldiers Flanking Betty at the Hoff Brau

A number of American soldiers came into the Hof Brau, spied us sitting at the table and joined us. We had a terrific time talking with them and reminiscing about the States. Later, we walked around Munich together and learned they were headed for Berlin the next day. A large convoy of American soldiers was going to build a wall to separate Berlin from Western Germany. I asked them how they felt about what they were about to do, and all three said they were afraid of a major conflict and they might die or be injured. My heart went out to them as they left, wondering if they would live or die in the next several days. As we left Munich, the Autobahn was crowded with Army conveys headed east to Berlin.

I arrived home, broke up with Curtis and was heartbroken for a long time. Then I discovered it was difficult talking normally to one of my best friends, Taso Vrenios. It was during my senior year that we fell in love.

Elizabeth and Taso Vrenios, Christmas 1966

170

Traveling with Pop
1961

(Betty)

When I graduated from the University of the Pacific, I knew I needed further education for what I wanted to do in life. Pop took me aside and explained he could no longer afford to help me and I would have to find my own way to pay for it. When I realized what that meant, I gulped and began to write graduate programs asking for admission with assistantships. I wanted to go to UCLA but the dean informed me that I could not get an assistantship until I had been in the program a year, and then it would be a partial one. This arrangement was impossible for me. When I applied to Elizabeth Spelt's alma mater, Northwestern, I was accepted with a full assistantship. The program was on the quarter system so I could finish my master's degree in a year, if I really concentrated. I was unsure about what to do for the rest of the finances, but trusted something would happen. I might be able to get a part time job.

Pop decided to drive me to school. It was a long and difficult drive from California to Chicago in his VW. He loaded my belongings in his truck and we set off. This was the first time I had been alone for a length of time with him and I truly enjoyed his calm energy and his "matter of fact" manner. Each evening we would look for an inexpensive motel, and cheap cafes by the highway.

We stopped along the way and visited Pop's relatives whom I had never met. His sister, Alice who died in 1942, had ten children who at this date ranged in age from forty three to fifty nine. Their children, the Hill clan, were scattered all over the mid-west. We stopped to see Albert Hill in Wyoming, and the Rodewald clan in Nebraska. Pop's sister, Sylvia and her husband, Ed had a ranch near Seneca. Sylvia had the same features as my father, except hers had wrinkles on them and were blackened by the sun. Her slim figure was covered with a housedress and her sinewy arms, bony and angular seemed to gesticulate constantly. She possessed an energy and confidence that was extraordinary. Compared to her, Pop seemed a bit shy. While I was there, Ed took me up in his small two-seater plane. We flew around the ranch and surrounding area. This was the first time I had experienced such a flight and felt exhilarated as I saw the fields and houses spread out below, small and orderly – roads much like I remembered creating as a child in my games. It gave me a sense of belonging I had never felt before. I learned later he died when this same plane crashed near the farm.

We stopped briefly to visit Pop's nephew Howard in Denver and I was appalled at the squalor of their house and yard. The children were playing in the dirt, barefoot and ragged. The house was a tiny place with animals roaming freely through the open front door the screen door was hanging by one hinge. The floor was littered with diapers and trash. They made no attempt to offer us a cup of coffee or tea. After a short visit, I was glad to leave.

We arrived at Northwestern and stopped at the housing office, because I needed to find out where I was to live. I anticipated I would receive names of places where graduate students lived off campus, and we would inquire about their availability. I walked into the office and the Dean of housing, asked my name and I was surprised she knew who I was. When I said that we had just arrived and I had no place to stay, she asked if I was interested in being a graduate resident. I would have full room and board in exchange for being responsible for my floor. My assignment would be in the Orrington apartments, one half block away from the building they called *the White Elephant,* which housed the music classes. This was the moment I began to see my path being laid out for me. An extraordinary good fortune had fallen into my lap.

After we put my suitcases and boxes in my room and had a bite to eat in a restaurant across the street, Pop climbed into his truck and headed for home. I was surprised at how quickly we were able to get me settled as I thought we would have a day to say goodbye. There was a lump in my throat and I cried. I felt small and lonely as I stood on the Evanston sidewalk watching Pop's truck disappear down the road. This was my first time out of California and leaving a member of the family. At that moment I felt the profundity of separation and the beginning of a new life.

Pop with his VW Truck (1961)

Singing for Supper
1965-92

(Betty)

I spent my adult life pursuing my heart's desire – singing and teaching. Taso and I sang in Summer stock for two years before we went to Santa Fe Opera as apprentices. Summer stock was at the Wagon Wheel Playhouse in Warsaw, Indiana where we performed five shows a summer. We rehearsed the show during the day, and performed another in the evening. In some shows we performed lead roles, and in others we did bit parts, or chorus. There was never time to do laundry or even sleep, but we loved every minute. I was fortunate to have several leads: Funny Thing Happened on the Way to the Forum, Fantastiks, Paint Your Wagon, Boys from Syracuse, Wonderful Town, and 110 in the Shade.

While we were there, Mom and Aunt Mayme visited us on their way back from Finland. Mayme confided in me that she would never travel with Mom again. I wasn't surprised because it was always difficult for Mom to maintain calm when she was traveling. She became impossible over trifling events. While they were there, the weather warmed up more than usual and in those days there was no such thing as an air conditioner. When we rehearsed at the playhouse we often ran a fan behind a bucket of water, which cooled off the air. Any time we had to sit on the stage in staging we would leave a puddle of water. It was rather funny to see the stage when we finished, filled with spots of water tracing all the places we had been during rehearsal.

At home one evening during this particularly hot spell, I got up to get a glass of water in the middle of the night and bumped into Mom wandering around the house stark naked. I was startled that she would walk around when anyone could see her, especially Taso. At one point Taso couldn't stand her complaining and arguing so he said he had to go to the theater. Mom told me when he left that she knew he was going to meet someone and I should watch out for him. She said whatever was in her head and most of the time it was thoughtless, cruel and angry.

1967

At Indiana University when I wanted to impress my new voice teacher, I tried to "do more than was expected." When he suggested I learn the six Brahms opus 95 songs, I learned and memorized them in German seven days later for the next lesson but I was not able to show him what I did, because during my lesson I never got past the first page of music.

*

After our stint at summer stock and Santa Fe, we returned to Indiana University to finish up our last year in graduate school. When the next summer arrived, Taso found himself touring with Sara Caldwell and her traveling opera company. I had a choice to remain at Indiana for a year or find something else to do. I didn't make up my mind until the last minute – leave and find a solid job somewhere. I went into the placement office at Indiana and talked with the gentleman there. It was now June. "What can I do for you, Betty," he asked.

"I've decided I want to teach at a university full time and find a job for the fall. It should be on the East Coast."

He sat back and laughed. "You have got to be kidding me, " he jibed. "All those jobs were gone last February. There aren't any such jobs available. Besides, you haven't any previous experience."

I held my ground. "Well, should one come up, please let me know about it. I really want to begin teaching this next year." He dismissed me skeptically and said he would let me know, but he didn't sound encouraging.

About three weeks later my phone rang. It was the placement office. "I don't know how you did it, but there is one job which has come through this week. It is a tenure track, voice performance position, and it is in Washington D.C. at American University. Everybody and his uncle will be applying so you better get your application in quickly."

I rushed to make a tape to send to the university along with my resume, transcripts and application and held my breath, as I knew several people at the university with more experience than I, had applied. A short time later I received a letter: I was one of the finalists and was asked to come to Washington DC for a final interview.

I wasn't the least bit nervous, and enjoyed the process of flying to D.C. and talking with the faculty. They offered me the job and later I heard why. The head of the voice department, James McLain, said, "Anyone who can sing *Depuis le Jour* as you do, certainly knows how to teach."

I was astounded to be offered the first job I applied for. I was gratified it was in Washington D.C. where my aunt and uncle, Arlene and Onnie Lattu were living. They were my only relatives outside of California and they lived three blocks from the university. I could see I was meant to go there. I remained there for 34 years. When I retired in 2001, I was the recipient of the faculty honor for outstanding service to the university.

Whenever I had a chance, I performed. I managed to perform the leads in Music Man, The Red Mill and Carousel and several other musicals and operas. My singing enabled me to meet great people such as Myrna Loy, Ned Rorem, Virgil Thompson, President Clinton, and Ambassadors from all over the world. I sang in Europe, Finland, Japan, Peru, Scandinavia, and across the US. My mentor, Elie Siegmeister was instrumental in my career, and I became the foremost interpreter of his contemporary music. I sang with ensembles and orchestras over the country. I've recorded his songs on several labels and had many pieces written for me.

1989

One of the most touching times of my performing was shortly after Nick was killed on the Pan Am Flight on December 21st. I appeared in Carnegie Recital Hall in New York in early March, performing some of Elie Siegmeister's music with a baritone, Jim Jivore. They were cycles of his and one of the works was a group of songs entitled *To My Children*. I could manage to sing all of the eight songs despite my state of mind, except for the last song in the cycle entitled *Goodbye,* which was a mother, saying goodbye to her child. The words were particularly touching: *Goodbye, Goodbye, I'm going away. Next morning will come quite without me. What will you say to the morning after that comes without me? Here is a kiss I put on each eye, weightless as love but will they stay? Here is a touch on your laughing mouth. Goodbye, I'm going away.*

When we were rehearsing in New York that afternoon in the hall, I began singing the song and broke down in tears. I looked at Alan Mandel who was at the piano and he was crying as well. The composer who was in the audience was choked up and croaked out – "Try it again. I'm sure you can do it". I tried again and when I came to the words "Goodbye", I simply could not sing them without crying, and Alan couldn't play it without tears. Elie insisted that we retain the song, so that evening I summoned up my courage and when I got to the passage "goodbye", I thought about peanut butter sandwiches and being hungry. I managed to sing that last note, but my voice quavered and the tears were there. I'm sure the audience had no idea why I was so emotional.

Professor Venereas Greets the President (1992)

1992

When President Clinton was in his first year as president he was slated to give his first foreign policy address at American University. As I had led the audience in the Star Spangled Banner for more than 20 years, they asked me to lead the audience in the national anthem for his address. No one at the university would unequivocally state whether he was definitely coming, or whether the event would truly take place. They "suggested" that we arrive at the auditorium before 8:00 and wait to see if he would arrive. I felt he wouldn't come, and

all this was for show, so I rolled out of bed and didn't bother to wash my hair or prepare myself particularly well. I drove to the campus and went to the waiting room somewhat disheveled. As I suspected, we waited more than three hours for the event to occur (or not). I was about ready to leave, when we were told that the event would begin in twenty minutes, and the president was on his way to the campus in upper northwest D.C. from the White House. I gulped, ran down to the women's room and combed my hair as best I could and put on
make-up. I had just finished when they urged me to hurry, as it was time to go in. I telephoned my

175

brother Don, and my mother to tell them what was happening. Still not anticipating the importance of the situation, I felt pretty confident and casual. At that point someone handed me a piece of music (which I had never seen before and which was the school song) and told me that they wanted me to teach it to everyone in the audience to sing. As I had taught classes before, still I wasn't concerned. I greeted President Clinton in the hallway and shook his hand and was impressed by his magnetic charisma. We entered the hall as the platform party and I saw the audience was packed into the large auditorium. I had never seen so many people there before. Spread across the entire auditorium was a large bank of TV cameras set up to catch this "once in a lifetime" event.

Everything went smoothly until the president of the University, Harold Duffy stood up and introduced me. He was notorious for not remembering names. "Ladies and Gentlemen" he announced, "May I present Professor Venereas who will lead us in the national anthem." It was all I could do to keep from laughing out loud at being compared to a venereal disease in front of the major news work networks that would spread my moniker across the country.

I had no idea the broadcast would go beyond our own local stations, but my brother Don called me up that evening from California and asked for "Professor Venereas," so I knew it had gone out across the country. Then I called my mother to see if she had seen it and she hadn't bothered to turn on her television to watch. What a shame – she might have enjoyed it.

Raising My Katzenjammer Kids
1976-77

(Betty)

Raising Nick and Chris, there were times when I had to take the boys with me when I rehearsed or when I sang. There were many times I wasn't able to get a baby sitter and Taso was gone a great deal on the road. One day I had to sing a group of songs *The Spohr Cycle with Clarinet* and had no baby-sitter. I was to perform in a large space with a balcony.

When I arrived, I looked into their eyes sternly and asked, "Where do you want to sit? It has to be where I can see you at all times." They looked around and simultaneously both of them pointed to the balcony. A short time later when I entered to sing, there were my boys sitting in the first row of the balcony. I was proud to have firmly stressed the seriousness of the situation. They giggled and waved at me as I opened my music and began to sing. No sooner had I begun, when, they climbed over the balcony and begin to swing on the outside of the railing. It didn't matter how sternly I looked at them or willed them back inside, they wouldn't budge. They cavorted and giggled for my entire song. When I finished and bowed to the applause, I saw them climb back inside and run. It took me twenty minutes to find them and cool off.

Because my life was busy, schedules were often controlled by baby sitters. When a sitter canceled at the last minute, I brought them with me to the university to sit through a master's recital,

177

or an opera rehearsal. When they sat through a recital, their favorite trick was to roll a soda can or marbles from the back row to the front. This was easy as the floor was sloped from the back of the auditorium to the front. All they had to do was let the marble or can go and it would travel all the way from the back to the front of the recital hall. The singer would be singing Schumann or Bach to the accompaniment of rrum rrum rrum all the way across the auditorium.

When I directed operas at the university, I felt Nick and Chris should be involved, so I put them in the chorus. Blow's *Venus and Adonis* had a cherubic chorus and I cast them with several of their friends as angels. They were to enter in cherub costumes which were little supplies with white tights and dance in a circle with their arms over their heads singing L…O…V…E…. During the performance, Chris had trouble with his tights, which kept slipping down. In desperation he reached down and held them up with one hand while trying to go through the dance. His tights continued to slip lower and lower until they were around his ankles. Later, I heard pandemonium backstage and rushed out to find the group of my little "angels" running up and down the hall having a powder fight.

The Powder Fight Gang: Nick and Chris in the Second Row

The last time I put them in an opera chorus, they were at the age where mischievousness is the norm. They were cast as 19th century Italian choirboys in *Cavalleria Rusticana*. They knew all the choruses by heart, and at night when I put them to bed I would hear them both singing the music at the top of their lungs from their respective bedrooms. On the night of the performance, they were well behaved during the procession behind the Catholic Bishop as it threaded its way through the audience. When the group arrived on stage, big bubbles appeared out of their mouths. They were all chewing bubble gum! I sneaked down to the foot of the stage and hissed at them, but they knew they had the upper hand and short of going up on the stage myself and hauling them off, I couldn't do anything. This was the last time I included them in operas.

One evening they begged me to let them sleep in a tent in the back yard. I set them up with the necessities of "camping," sleeping bags, snacks, flashlights and comic books. They settled down quickly, and after I checked on them, I retired for the night. Around 2:00 in the morning, I heard the doorbell ring and raced downstairs to see a police officer with two little boys - one in each hand. "Do these belong to you?" he asked. I thought for a moment, and then reluctantly I acknowledged they did. Apparently they had walked a half-mile up the road with several of their friends to the Safeway Store on the corner of Connecticut Avenue, a very busy street. They made their way to the top of the store and threw firecrackers off the roof at the traffic below. Someone called the police and a S.W.A.T. team arrived by helicopter with guns looking for the "criminals." Imagine what they thought when they saw five small boys huddled in the corner of the roof.

Elizabeth in Helsinki Concert

An Opportunity to Travel
1978-90
(Betty)

My singing enabled me to travel to several countries, some exotic. I was able to go to Finland with the help of Uncle Onnie, to sing in East Berlin at a festival with Alan Mandel who was my colleague at the university, tour Europe and Scandinavia with a chamber ensemble group, and was invited by the State Department to sing in Peru as a representative of the United States.

Peru (1978)

When I arrived in Lima on the plane, it was one o'clock in the morning and the airport was deserted. There was no one to meet me. I communicated with the Cultural Attaché the week before, and explained I was arriving at eleven PM. I did not realize that all international communications regarding time were on a twenty-four hour basis, and everyone assumed I was arriving at eleven in the morning. I didn't speak enough Spanish to make myself understood well, and depended on someone at the airport to speak English. There was no one. There was a bus to downtown Lima, so I climbed on board with my suitcases and was deposited at one of the downtown hotels. I checked in, and slept like a log. The next day I called the embassy and informed them where I was. They sent someone to pick me up and take me to the family with whom I was to stay. I was chagrined at my naiveté about telling time.

In Peru I was scheduled to sing a recital in two cities and a concert with the orchestra in Lima.

180

I wanted to sing something distinctively American and made an arrangement of some Moravian songs for orchestra. The night I sang the concert in Lima, I took a cab across the city to where I was singing. At the rehearsal that afternoon, I asked "What time should I arrive this evening? The concert begins at seven."

"You can arrive around eight. The audience will not be there until then." As is the custom in the United States, the performer arrives one half hour before the concert, and I did not believe the advice I was given. I was there at six thirty. I arrived to find the building still locked up. The clarinetist was there as well, and he crawled in a window to let me in as we waited for everyone else to arrive. The conductor was right – the audience began arriving about eight o'clock, and the concert began approximately one and a quarter hours after the published time.

When I left to go home, I took a cab in the dark, again across the city. Several were lined up in front of the building eagerly seeking fares. I must have been quite a sight, dressed to the nines in my evening gown with an armful of flowers and full stage make up. The driver of the second cab approached me aggressively and took me by the arm to lead me to his car. When I climbed in, the driver from the first cab stormed over and threatened my cabbie, arguing and hitting the roof and windows. I was about to get out as the confrontation was loud and hostile, but my cabbie told me to stay put. He pealed out in front of the man, who was left standing in the road shaking his fist. I saw him run for his cab and before I knew it, he was chasing us down the street trying to push us off the road. My cabbie drove like a maniac, cutting corners, racing up the streets, ducking into alleys all while the first car was on his tail. This mad chase continued for several miles as we crossed the city, while I cowered in the back seat with pictures running through my mind of headlines in the paper back home "local soprano dies in Peruvian car crash". Before I was dropped off at my destination, we managed to elude our pursuer. I vowed to always take the first cab in the cue.

I gave a concert in a cloistered monastery in Arequipa. My concert was to be the first time in several centuries that outsiders were allowed inside the building. A lovely grand piano was available which had been shipped down from the foggy damp climate of Lima to the arid desert of the valley where Arequipa was situated. We rehearsed in the lovely stone chapel where I was to sing, and I noticed that the piano was so out of tune as to be virtually useless. Both the pianist and I anxiously inquired about the tuning and were assured that "the piano tuner would be there right after our rehearsal and would prepare the instrument for our concert."

Later that evening when we returned, the audience, which anticipated hearing the "American soprano", had packed the monastery awaiting our concert. The ancient stonewalls reverberated with the excited sounds of the crowd as I walked out. The pianist adjusted his tails, sat and prepared to strike the first chord of the music I was about to sing. I had chosen a declamatory piece by Handel, which was a rousing beginning to the concert: *Let the Bright Seraphim.* It begins with a very loud D major chord. What I heard next was something I never experienced before. The lovely D major chord slid immediately to C# major and then disintegrated to something near the key of C, and eventually became a cacophony of sound.

Apparently the pegs of the piano had been shaved to allow the tuning of the instrument while the piano was in Lima. This was done because the wooden pegs, swollen from the humidity couldn't fit into the holes. In Arequipa the pegs shrank and dried out. They slipped and couldn't hold the strings of the piano in place. As a result the pitches couldn't be sustained. Since the piano had been shipped to Arequipa especially for the concert, this was the first time it had been played in the monastery. No one realized this would happen. The pianist immediately began to play as softly as he could to maintain the sound as long as he could. The music that evening sounded very strange.

I traveled to Cuzco, as I wanted to see Machu Picchu before I left Peru. My flight arrived in the late morning and since I didn't speak much Spanish, I decided to wait until all the passengers who crowded around the luggage were gone. Meanwhile, cab drivers walked around the crowd asking in Spanish if anyone needed a ride. Each time they asked I shook my head and they moved on.

I turned around and without thinking answered, "Yes," confident this was the right cab driver. He walked to the front of the swarm of people, retrieved my suitcase and inquired, "Do you have a place to stay?"

I replied, "I don't, and I need a suggestion."

"I know of a hotel in downtown Cuzco where the walls of the building were built by the Incans centuries ago." I climbed in the cab, a little anxious as I was alone in a strange country, and could not speak to make myself understood. He took me to a charming hotel in downtown Cuzco and spoke with the clerk at the desk to help me check in. "It would be good for you to sleep for an hour because of the altitude. I will be back at three to pick you up and take you around Cuzco to see the sights."

I was feeling the effects of the extremely high altitude, so I went to sleep as he suggested. I was waiting in the lobby at three o'clock and the driver arrived promptly. I was astonished, as I was used to the careless attitude of cab drivers in New York. That afternoon he took me around the hills, helped me bargain with local venders and even took me to the train station to buy my ticket on the train for the next morning to Machu Picchu. I spent several wonderful hours enjoying the sights. When we finished and arrived back to the hotel, he asked "What are you doing this evening?"

"Aha," I thought, "Here is the kicker!" I assumed that he was going to make a move on me, but trusting my instinct, replied, "Nothing. Why do you ask?"

"There is a program of native dancers tonight in the city. It will be very exciting, and you should see it while you are here. I will pick you up at quarter to eight and take you." Cautiously, I agreed. He was at the hotel at exactly seven forty-five and drove me to the hall where the dancers were. "I will be here waiting outside the door when they are finished. You can meet me here." Having left me off, his cab disappeared down the street. He was as good as his word, and when the concert over over I spied him through the crowd of people at the front curb waiting to pick me up. "I will be at the hotel early in the morning to get you to the Machu Picchu tour. See you then," he said as he dropped me off that evening.

The next morning I wasn't surprised he was waiting for me. He took me to the train with the promise he would be back when it returned from Machu Picchu.

The train was rambling and slow and weaving lazily through the Amazon. It stopped in the middle of the jungle and I assumed people were getting on at that remote location. Several people got off to stretch their legs, and re-boarded ten minutes later. We ambled further until we came to a screeching stop. Ahead of us was a landslide over the tracks. We got out and scrambled past the slide where a second train was waiting to take us the rest of the way to Machu Picchu. When we arrived three hours later at the fabled Inca ruins, we hiked up a steep hill to get to the city. Llamas roamed freely everywhere, hissing if you came too close. I spent a glorious afternoon climbing the hills, investigating the stonework, the water system, the ingenious building techniques and the spectacular view of the Amazon jungle.

When we returned to the train in the evening, we were fatigued from the high altitude and the strenuous climbing. We meandered back through the jungle on the same route as the morning, and stopped at the clearing in the Amazon. Again, people got off to stretch their legs, but this time the train pulled out almost immediately leaving ten people on the dirt road at the edge of the jungle. I looked back in amazement and saw panic in the astonished faces of the people standing outside the train. The train continued on and the figures became smaller and smaller in the distance. I wondered what those passengers did that evening in the jungle with nothing around them, waiting for the train, which would not arrive until the next day.

Machu Picchu, Peru (1978)

As expected, the cab driver was waiting for me when I returned. He made an appointment to pick me up early in the morning to take me to the airport. On the drive out of the city, we passed houses that looked as if they were in ruins. "Do you see those houses? They were destroyed by soldiers the last time the people went on strike against the government." I could see bullet holes in the walls, and portions of homes in ruins from evident devastation. "I am the head of the cab association and next week I am leading the revolution for the workers as I did several years ago. The police will be there with guns to stop us. I don't know what will happen." I realized that he might be killed during this revolt, as the government was suppressing insurrection. With a lump in my throat I said goodbye, knowing I would never know what happened to him.

Japan (1989)

I traveled to Japan with the Inoue Ensemble to sing a world premiere in Tokyo with the Tokyo Symphony as well as to give several concerts, radio broadcasts and master classes. I found Tokyo very crowded and confusing. There were neon signs everywhere as well as loud music and blaring announcements. The policemen, taxi cab drivers and workers all wore white gloves to protect themselves. All the cars were new, as the taxation system was the opposite of ours: the older the car, the higher the taxes. As the car ages, the taxes become so prohibitive that everyone trades them in. Cars were equipped with a small light on the top of the roof. If a driver went over the speed limit, the policemen who were stationed all over the city could merely notate the license plate in order to serve the fine.

I stayed with the other two musicians outside Tokyo, which was about an hour's train ride into the center of the city. One day when we were to have a rehearsal at the Tokyo Conservatory at the center of Tokyo, Kosito Inoue, who was in charge of putting the program together, left early, and I traveled into Tokyo by myself for the rehearsal. Before she left, I asked her to write down directions in Japanese so that I could present it to the cab driver in order to get to the conservatory. I knew it would be impossible to ask for the conservatory in Japanese. She wrote them on a piece of paper, which I stowed away in my purse.

I studied the Japanese characters very carefully at each stop of the train so that I could identify my final station. Finally I saw what I thought was the correct stop and debarked. I dashed up to the street with the precious paper in my hand. Hailing a cab, I proudly gave him the paper and settled down in the back seat. Turning around, he gesticulated and spoke rapidly in Japanese. This was my worst nightmare. I pointed deliberately to the Japanese characters on the paper hoping for a smile of recognition, but he continued to shake his head and argue. For several minutes I insisted he follow what it said on the paper by pointing and nodding. Finally he shrugged his shoulders and pulled the cab slowly out into the traffic. He drove for quite a long time and I kept my eye on the meter. When I saw that the fare was edging toward ninety dollars, I knew I could no longer afford to keep going. I told him to stop, paid him, and stepped out of the cab, penniless.

I found myself in a strange part of the city, which was dark and foreboding. Remembering advice I heard from people that everyone in Tokyo speaks English, I stopped those I met and asked for directions to a police station. I discovered that few people in Tokyo speak or understand our English language. Finally one gentleman pointed to a building several blocks away and, relieved, I ran up the block to find the station. By now I was very late to the orchestral rehearsal. The police did speak English, and offered me a ride to the conservatory. Unable to contain my curiosity, I handed the paper to one of the officers asking, "What does the note say?"

He took it and read with a puzzled look. Handing the paper back to me, he said, "It says the third column on the left.'"

Elizabeth Vrenios in Japan (1989)

East Berlin (1990)

I had the opportunity to go to East Berlin with Alan Mandel to sing in a festival featuring the two of us. It was moving to be in Berlin close to the removal of the Berlin wall, when I had been in Germany years before as the wall was being constructed. The performance was in a beautiful renovated barn, which was somewhat isolated. It was a retreat available for guest artists and musicians in Germany who wished to compose or present their music in performance. Alan and I were to present a contemporary music festival, and I was busy preparing several concerts of unusual contemporary music.

When we finished the three days of performances, we traveled back to Amsterdam by auto and passed through portions of East Berlin. I was devastated at what I saw. The streets and buildings were deserted and in disrepair. The buildings were the same weathered-gray with darkened interiors. I felt I was on a movie set depicting Nazi Germany. On the West-German side of the wall, the contrast was markedly different. People were laughing and singing, stores had windows full of colorful goods and buildings were painted and well lit.

*

We were in Amsterdam overnight before we were to take the plane home, and decided to walk through the city. I heard about the famous red-light district of the city and we walked there to see what it was all about. I was embarrassed that we were going there, but Alan in his own intrepid way, was not. He stopped every two blocks to ask directions. Each time he approached someone, I turned my back and pretended I wasn't with him. We arrived at the district, which was everything that

185

people had said. Women posed in small rooms with enormous windows lining the street in all manners of dress – some costumed, some with very little on - enticing the passersby to come into the building. There was a glow of lights, which were literally "red lights". I had never seen anything like this and put the experience down as part of my "musical education."

Elizabeth Vrenios in Berlin (19??

Self Portrait of Nick Vrenios in Scotland

The Pan Am Bombing

December 21, 1988

JOY
Elizabeth Kirkpatrick Vrenios

There is no accounting for the unaccustomed joy
Returning to land in the dust at my feet –
A multicolored bird, exhilarated by its flight,
Or the gentle touch of the butterfly,
Kissing my arm as it flutters by,
Invoking me into a warm embrace of the sun.

Should I run inside and dress for this invitation?
What do you require from me to stay in this light?
The joy permeates my skin,
warming my stone of a heart.

Joy is the prodigal return of a son,
long buried in the ground,
elated by his flight.
It is the arrival at my front gate
of a battered mustard-yellow Nissan
announcing its noisy arrival
With rattles and bangs...
such music to accompany my beating heart.
Joy races up the steps to yell his arrival,
as rubbing my eyes,
I rouse myself from a nap,
Taken to escape an afternoon of despair.

Joy comes to the solitary pilot landing his craft on home soil.
It comes to the singer in the midst of a beautiful melody.
The child with a ball,
The water bubbling in the fountain,
The chimes as they release their sound in the wind.
The petals of a flower stretching its fingers to the sun,
The book about to be read,
The glass, tired of holding the wine,
The stone in the sun.

The Darkest Day of the Year
December 21, 1988

(Betty)

Our oldest son, Nick had an obvious relish of life, which gave me light and sunshine – and laughter when I needed it most. His sense of humor mirrored mine, only with more imagination and relish. While away at Syracuse University, I would learn of his adventures – doing his homework in the elevator so that he could talk to his friends on the way up and down, traveling to Canada on week ends, playing his guitar to make money for his trip home. In many ways he exhibited the fearlessness of youth – unfettered and joyous. In the fall of his sophomore year he went on a skiing trip in Colorado with some of his friends and had an accident, which put him in a cast for several months. The winter term at Syracuse was just beginning and he decided that it was too difficult for him to maneuver the hills and snow in crutches so he opted to stay at home for a semester. What a joy that was for me, for I was able to get to know him. We connected, talked, and in those few months I began to know my beautiful, energetic son quite well.

He decided to go to London in the fall Semester while at Syracuse University as several of his friends were going and he wanted to pursue his newly declared degree in photography. We applied and even though he was technically not a junior, he was accepted into the program and went. His joie de vivre was evident. He rode his skateboard all over London, making friends everywhere he went. He carried his guitar with him and never hesitated to sit down and play for anyone who wanted to hear him. When he was in London studying as an exchange student, his teacher tells of a time when the class went to Penzance to take pictures. When it was time to get back on the bus, Nick wasn't there. He went back to look for him and found him on the street corner, playing guitar with a homeless man, helping him to fill up his hat with money. The teacher had noticed the homeless man earlier in the day and when he passed the beggar in the gathering dusk, dropped a rather large coin in the hat, thinking in his mind that he was playing better than he had earlier in the day – not realizing that the beggar was Nick.

"Brrt Brrt," the phone was ringing, and just as we were ready to go. Taso and I were headed to New York to pick up Nicky who had finished in London. Everything was ready for him. I had worked hard the last few days, finishing up exams at the university and giving some papers a briefer glance than usual in order to steal some time to prepare for Nick's homecoming. The stockings hung carefully on the fireplace as they had been since the boys were children: Five with the names Chris, Nick, Dad and Mom and an S for Sparky (our miniature Schnauzer). These homemade – green and white checked stockings with red lettering awkwardly sewn on were created in a time when money was tight and I had to make them myself. Goodies were baked and ready and I had wrapped most of the gifts. The candles and greenery were set out. All that was left was adding family. This was going to be a special Christmas. We were collectively excited to have our long departed son return home.

Chris was off, mowing lawns and had come to the decision to finally break a year's long silence between them. He also was anxiously awaiting Nick's return. I was bursting with joy to see

Nick again and to hear of his adventures. To see my two sons embrace again after such a long period of anger and rejection was a prayer about to be answered. I had missed the excitement that the two boys could spark in each other. Humor and adventure were always present when they were together. It seemed as if the long wait was over.

I rushed back up the walk, hurriedly fished my house keys from purse, and managed to pick up the phone on the 5th ring. It was Nick's voice: "Hi Mom, How are you?"

"Nick, Dad and I were just leaving for New York to pick you up." We were going to stay overnight and pick him up the next day at the airport. "How are you?"

"Oh, I'm OK. I just got back from Scotland and something happened there."

"What was it, Sweetheart?" My stomach flipped over in anxiety.

"Oh, it's too long a story. I'll tell you when I see you. I just wanted to hear your voice."

"Do you want to speak to Dad?"

"Sure."

I ran to the door and yelled "It's Nick!" Want to talk to him?"

"No, tell him I will see him when he arrives. We'd better get going."

I ran back and briefly talked with him giving him our love and wishing him a safe journey the next day.

When I returned to the car, my body ached with anxiety and longing for my eldest son. How much I had missed him. I could picture him sitting in the back seat telling us everything on our return back to DC.

The drive to New York seemed longer than usual. We were both impatient for the time to pass so we could see Nick. That evening we walked up Park Avenue and looked in the windows at the displays, saw the tree at Rockefeller Center, and managed to find a tripod for Nick to complete the complement of gifts we had already wrapped. The weather was unusually warm that evening. We wore light jackets and the festive mood of the crowd seemed to add to the sparkle and excitement of the homecoming.

The following day we left for Kennedy airport, not allowing enough time to get there ahead of time. The classical music station was on, as it usually was, and I was hoping it would calm Taso who was becoming increasingly anxious and defensive, fighting the extraordinary heavy volume of the rush hour traffic. As we rushed up to the terminal, Taso said "You run out and see if you can meet him at the gate. I'll double park and wait for you."

I ran into the terminal, scanning the arrival board to see when the Pan Am 103 flight would arrive. "Darn! It wasn't there. I must have missed it." Panicking for fear I would miss him, I ran up to the Pan Am counter. It seemed crowded with an unusual number of people. A crowd of people was gathered at the far right of the area, cordoned off so they couldn't cross into the larger area. There didn't appear to be anyone at the ticket counter. Bright lights from TV cameras were everywhere. It appeared to me as if they were making a TV commercial.

I ran over to the group of agents standing around talking in a huddle. "Excuse me" I said, afraid to interrupt an important conversation, but aware of the TV cameras. "Can you tell me at what gate Flight 103 is arriving?"

One agent turned and eyed me suspiciously. "Why do you want to know?"

Indignantly and impatiently I answered, "Because I'm meeting my son there. I'm late. Has it arrived?"

The agents glanced at each other and without saying a word, one of them grabbed my arm and began walking very rapidly to a side door. "Where are you taking me? What's going on?" I demanded. Suddenly, I saw out of the corner of my eye someone running full tilt toward us with a camera. The second agent turned back to block them while the first agent shoved me through the double doors. I found myself on an elevator standing in the middle of four very tall men, feeling very tiny.

"We would like to take you upstairs. Something has happened."

"What do you man? Was the plane hijacked?" In those days stories abounded of hijacked planes being diverted to a different arrival while the pilots were held hostage at gunpoint." This was the worst possible scenario that I could imagine.
The group looked at each other and glanced down in embarrassment. "Will someone tell me what happened?"

"Someone upstairs will talk to you." I was ushered into a very large room teaming with people

"What's going on?" Anxiety was creeping up the back of my neck.

"Is there anyone with you?"

"Yes", I replied. "My husband. He's waiting in the car double parked outside."

"I'll send someone down to get him. They will park your car for you." He led me to a curved large leather sofa. "Someone will be over to talk to you soon."

"Can you tell me what happened?"

"There has been some kind of an accident," and he turned on his heels leaving me alone. I looked around and could see people who seemed to be sitting in groups talking. There were agents with most of the small clusters of two and three, talking. Here and there I heard a sob. After quite a long time, a gentleman approached me. "What is happening?" I asked again.

"We don't know – only that there has been some kind of accident."

"Is my son all right?"

"We don't know. Give me his name and we will check to see if his name is on the manifold. He may have missed the plane or is on another one." He left and again I was alone to wonder what had happened.

I closed my eyes to feel the essence of what was happening and to feel the presence of Nick. All I could sense was calm. There was no panic at the center of me, simply calm. I interpreted this as a good sign.

Taso came running in with another man who led him over to where I was sitting. "What's going on?"

That's what I've been trying to find out!"

The agent returned and sat. "There was an explosion", he said slowly.

"Was the plane on the ground or in the air?" I asked.

He look down and said quietly "In the air."
Taso looked questioningly at me. "He's gone," I whispered. At that moment, I had the distinct

sensation of Nick swooping down from the air, past us and out of the window. It felt real and as if his soul was coming to say one last goodbye.

We called home and Chris answered. "Mom", what's going on? The house is full of people and I want them to go home. Is Nick all right?"

"No Darling, he's gone," I said. "If you feel you want people around you, then invite them to stay. Otherwise you can ask them to leave."

The officials asked us if we would like a hotel room for the night, and we said "yes", as we were in a state of shock. We were ushered to a very beautiful suite and the first thing we did was turn on the TV to find out what was going on. There we finally learned the story about the Pan Am crash and the destruction over Lockerbie. Everyone on the plane was killed as well as several people in Lockerbie.

We sat, stunned at what we saw, for none of this was relayed to us in the terminal. A panic started to rise in my chest. "We have to go home! Right now!" Taso nodded, "You're right, we should go." We left, telling the people at the desk that we needed to leave and began the torturous drive home. The night was clear, crisp and very cold. There wasn't a cloud in the sky and as we drove, the moon cast a strong light through the car windows, mocking us with its beauty. We couldn't talk. I closed my eyes and imagined Nick in the back seat riding with us asleep. I couldn't bring myself to the realization that our first born, our 'sunny Nick' was gone.

It took far longer than normal to make the drive from New York to Washington. The sun was coming up as we arrived at the beltway in Washington and we met some heavy morning traffic. It had now been about 12 hours since we heard the news.

Taso went upstairs to lie down, but I felt I needed a shower. I quickly showered, and as I was getting out and putting on my robe (about 7:00 am) the doorbell rang. I ran downstairs and there, standing on our front porch was a reporter. "May I talk with you Mrs. Vrenios?"

"No," I replied rubbing my head which felt numb, "we've just returned home and need to rest. Come back later."

A few moments later the doorbell rang a second time and a messenger handed me a letter from the president of American University, Richard Berendzen, expressing condolences.

We had a brief quiet period of about a half an hour when the phone began to ring. Every time we hung up, the phone rang again. It didn't stop for more than four days. People from St. George's Greek Church called, as did students, colleagues, friends, relatives, Nick's friends and as well as Chris's friends. One of the calls that morning was from Adelaide Whitaker insisting that she come over and help answer the phone. I tried to turn her down, but she insisted and arrived just in time to begin fielding the flood of people on the phone and at the door. She helped organize the students and friends who arrived to help and those who brought food.

Reporters arrived asking for interviews and students and friends of Chris and Nick flooded the house just to be there. I talked and talked to many, expressing my profound belief in the inevitability of events and expressing my belief that we had to accept events as they occurred. It was during these talks that I began to solidify my faith and verbalize my beliefs.

The day after the incident, one of Nick's friends came down from his room with an odd look on his face. When I asked what was wrong, he showed me a notebook with poetry scribbled in the margins. The poem was certainly prescient if not astounding.

"Such a brilliant ball of fire,
it showed with rainbow colors,
as it plumaged to the earth
in the dim blue sky.
It appeared significantly inspiring
as if to give my life meaning.
Wondrous and mysterious for I
Have never witnessed such a splendor."

The message of those few words couldn't be ignored! The description of the plane falling to the earth in flames is astounding. The dim blue sky signifies the fact that the plane fell in a rainstorm. This event certainly did give his life meaning and splendor.

The relatives from Canada arrived, as did Don and Shirley, and eventually, Kanella, Taso's sister, and her girls came. All we could bring ourselves to eat was avgholemono soup and chicken-vegetable soup for three weeks, feeding all those who came. Many brought food that we put out. It seemed as if we had a wake for Nick from December 22nd until Christmas Eve when it abruptly stopped. Chris, Taso and I found ourselves suddenly alone without the joy or impulse to open gifts. I decided to take the stockings down because I couldn't bear seeing them empty. They have never been put up again.

A Message from the Clouds
December 21, 1988

(Betty)

Taso, Chris and I went to Lockerbie in the spring in order to see some of the belongings that could not be identified. We had been sent various packages of belongings that were Nick's over the months preceding our visit. Each package brought a new anguish as we received his skateboard, items of clothing and his wallet and passport. All of them were distorted and damaged by the rainstorm that had occurred during the crash as well as the explosion, which covered everything with a dark ash. When we visited the "store" as the Scots call it, we didn't expect what we saw. Everywhere were mountains of objects taken from the plane, categorized and labeled. There were piles of belongings, not identifiable to anyone in the plane. Everything was water soaked and covered with the same dark ash.

We went to the area where they had the photographs, as we hadn't received any photos from the crash. Nicholas being a photography student surely would have had photos of his semester in London. The Scots had gathered all the rolls of film from the 270 passengers and developed each roll, matching each image to what they thought could have one of the victims. One of the officers came towards us carrying a stack of photos more than two feet high. I couldn't believe that there were that many photos from Nick's trip. On top of the pile was an 11x19 photograph, which was astounding! As we looked at the picture I could see the guards at the side whispering to each other and watching us closely. The picture was of Nicholas sitting on a rocky mountaintop surrounded by clouds, holding a Duars' Gin bottle. There was no damage to the picture. It was perfect as an art photo could be. This seemed impossible given the circumstances of the explosion and rain that had occurred. I asked the guard where they had found the photo. One of them went to the map that was on the wall and pointed to Lockerbie. "Here is the crash", he said. Pointing to the upper edge of Scotland, hundreds of miles away, next to the ocean, he exclaimed, "Here was where the photo was found. A hunter in the Umbrian forest caught it as it fell from the sky. He assumed that it belonged to the crash and sent it to us." The amazing thing was the photo had no drops of rain on it, had traveled several hundred miles high above the earth to this obscure forest next to the ocean, and recovered to be returned to us. If the photo had been ordinary, it would have been miracle enough. But this photo was a picture of Nicholas smiling on an outcrop surrounded by clouds, as if to say, "See! I'm all right."

Later that day, our host family from Lockerbie who was taking us around the area asked us if we wanted to see where Nicholas had fallen. We said "yes" and immediately set out to a meadow in the northern section of Lockerbie. After traveling over a narrow pathway and climbing over several "stiles" we came to the area where the part of the plane Nick had been in had fallen. They pointed over the field which now had been planted with a new crop - growing green and fresh, and said "There is where your son fell." My heart leaped into my throat and tears welled in my eyes as I imagined that horrible night several months earlier.

Chris wanted to stand where Nick had fallen and climbed over the fence. After trekking to the middle of the field, he looked back at us and a strange expression came over his face. "You need to come over here." I climbed over the fence to see what he was talking about and there on the old fence post covered with moss, someone had outlined "Nicholas" in nails on the post, in the place where he had fallen. There was no other name anywhere to be seen, only our son's name shone on that old piece of Scottish wood in an obscure field.

In the years since the tragedy many things have happened. New machinery has been installed in order to determine items a terrorist might use on our airplanes. Cameras and devices have been installed to identify explosives and baggage is now inspected. Aid and comfort have been instigated for those who have lost their families to a terrorist tragedy, and scholarships have been set up in the names of the lost passengers on that tragic flight. Syracuse has initiated twenty or more scholarships in the names of those fallen. Students are chosen from an essay written on terrorism and what it means in a changing world.

We have begun to connect to the world and have begun to make it a safer place because of those lost in that flight many years ago. There is an exchange program between Syracuse and Lockerbie with scholarships going to young Scottish students to enable them to travel to the United States in order to study. Many blessings have arisen from this tragedy. There have been art works created, music written, concerts given, scholarships awarded, photographs dedicated, and people helped the world over. A memorial has been set up in the National Cemetery. It is a cairn created out of stone from Scotland – a round monument created with 270 stones, each one representing a person lost on that tragic flight. I keep saying to myself that Nicholas had a hand in this. He could have lived his entire life and never made one-tenth the contribution to mankind as he has been able to do in his dying.

MARK LAWRENCE TOBIN
DAVID WILLIAM TRIMMER-SMITH
ALEXIA KATHRYN TSAIRIS
BARRY JOSEPH VALENTINO
ASAAD EIDI VEJDANY
MILUTIN VELIMIROVICH
NICHOLAS ANDREAS VRENIOS
PETER VULOU
RAYMOND RONALD WAGNER
JANINA JOZEFA WAIDO
THOMAS EDWIN WALKER
KESHA WEEDON
JEROME LEE WESTON

Bob's Wall

Bob & Kathleen

Robert Kirkpatrick Autobiography
1929- Present

(Bob)

I am a Mendocino County person. I was conceived at Glass Beach in Fort Bragg, but that's another story. My parents were caretakers of an isolated logging camp in the Redwoods. The only way in and out of the camp was via the Skunk Train. By February 11, 1929, my mother was pregnant with me and sensed that I'd be along shortly. My dad was out working in the woods so my mom had to take the Skunk Train to Fort Bragg by herself. She checked into the Fort Bragg General Hospital, now known as The Blue Whale Inn. I was born seven hours later. I have a pin, which says, "I was born in The Blue Whale Inn". I was only seven hours from having a pin that says, "I was born on the Skunk Train".

My parents moved to Healdsburg when I was a year old. My father took a job at the Basalt Rock Company. He eventually became a general contractor. My mother, a graduate of the Humboldt Normal School, taught at the local Grant, Litton, and Windsor schools. My brother, Don, and then my sister, Betty, joined the family. We grew up together. We played, worked and went to school.

In June of 1946, I graduated from Healdsburg High School. I joined the Navy the day after graduation because I had a terrible fight with my mother the night before. She was furious because I had worn a sport shirt under my graduation gown instead of a dress shirt and tie. Joining the Navy and leaving home seemed like a wise thing to do at the time. I was in the Navy for two years and visited the Philippines, China, Korea, Japan, Okinawa, Guam, Truk, and Hawaii. I learned something about the ways of the world.

After my discharge from the Navy, I attended Santa Rosa Junior College for a year and was set on being a dentist until I got a "C" in chemistry. At that point I switched my major to history and English, and was much happier. I transferred to U.C. Berkeley and graduated in 1952.

My mom was an immigrant, born in Finland, who entered the U.S. through Ellis Island in 1906. Learning to speak English well, and being an educated person were very important to her and subsequently to our whole family. I decided to go into education and received my teaching credential by 1953. My first job was at Las Lomas High School in Walnut Creek. The work was enjoyable and I was a good teacher.

I married Marilyn Schade in 1953, and fifteen months later Robert Sean was born. About this time, I realized that I could do a better job than the principal of my school and I began to work for my administrative credential at U.C. Berkeley. I took classes in the evenings, on weekends, and in the summers. In 1958, I earned my administrative credential.

I applied for an assistant principal-ship in Paradise, and was hired. At Paradise Junior/Senior High School, I was expected to handle the discipline, be the athletic director and athletic office manager, supervise the English, and history teachers, run the adult school, and coordinate student events. On top of everything else our daughter, Kathy, was born that first school year in Paradise. This was the beginning of a wonderful career that defined my identity and gave me the chance to support changes in education to benefit students for over thirty years.

During the spring of my first year as vice principal, a professor from Stanford stopped by my office and asked if I would be interested in attending an advanced summer session in administration at Stanford University. I fell in love with Stanford and became passionate about the school and its graduate program for educators. The people at Stanford offered to help with expenses if I would work for a doctoral degree. Who me? This offer made me feel excited and honored. I went back to Paradise for one more year and began making plans to start working for my doctorate in June of 1960.

We sold our home to pay the tuition to Stanford. I found a half time job as an administrative assistant in the Mountain View-Los Altos School District. I had another part time job working on a federal grant, titled "Voters and Their Schools." I took classes, and studied, studied, studied, and studied. I received my doctorate in educational administration in 1962.

Two of my professors, Dr. William O'dell and Dr. James McConnell had a consulting company for school districts. They asked me if I would like to work for them at O'dell McConnell and Associates. I was one of their associates and that meant I did the grunt work. I would do the enrollment projections, educational specifications for school buildings, budget analysis and other such tasks for the firm.

One of the districts that hired us was the Los Banos High School District. The federal government was going to build the San Luis Reservoir in the district. The district was expected to grow and they wanted to know how much. I interviewed the contractors, asked them how long would it take, how many people they were going to employ, how many were married, how many had kids, and where they would live? From this information, it looked as if the district would just about double in size. I helped the district develop the educational specifications for new schools to facilitate this enormous transition.

While I was working in Los Banos, the superintendent had a heart attack and decided to retire. I was getting a little tired of living in motels and applied for the job. I was hired as half-time superintendent for both the Los Banos Elementary School District and the Los Banos High School District. There were two boards, two offices, and two of everything else. I was thirty-four and the youngest superintendent in California.

My first job was hiring seventy-six new teachers under emergency conditions in June and July for them to be on board by the start of school in September. I did all of the interviews by myself, as I did not have the time, staff, or experience to set up interview committees. I organized and planned for school wide double sessions. I helped to plan and build a new high school, a new elementary school, remodeled one of the elementary schools, and converted the old high school into a junior high school. I also worked with the other two elementary districts that fed into the high school district. I helped unify all four districts into the new Los Banos Unified School District. I hired the first and second black teachers in the district and started building kindergarten through grade twelve curricula. Things were happening so fast, when I made the inevitable mistakes of the inexperienced, they quickly vanished in this blizzard of activity.

After six years of this exciting, interesting, and fast paced leadership, I applied for superintendent of the Merced Elementary School District. Again, I was surprised to be hired. This district was about four times the size of Los Banos and had plenty of support staff in the district office. Instead of doing almost everything by myself, I had help. This was a new experience.

The first job the board wanted me to do was to desegregate the school system. This was a good time to voluntarily desegregate. People across the United States were watching districts that attempted to do this. Sometimes these groundbreaking districts were criticized and sometimes they were congratulated. The federal government gave us two grants of one million dollars to help make the job easier. I remember school board meetings with five to seven hundred people in the audience.

The second job the board wanted me to do was to develop a unified sex education curriculum and implement the new Title IX regulations supporting gender equity. The audiences for this were not as big as the desegregation audiences but they were sizable. In addition I helped to plan and build a new middle school and remodel an elementary school. I started redoing the kindergarten through eighth grade curricula.

After twelve years in Merced, I found myself at a low point. I was tired and disillusioned. I was tired of feeding the dog, mowing the lawn, cleaning the swimming pool, and doing what I was doing at the District Office. I needed to reinvent my life. I started looking for another job, separated from my first wife, and bought a sports car. I applied for the job of Superintendent in Willits, and thanked my lucky stars when I got it. It felt like I had come home.

Before I moved to Willits, I knew I wouldn't be joining Rotary again. Keeping up eighteen years of perfect attendance had become a real chore, however, I wanted to be a part of the community. I applied for the opening on the Willits Cultural Arts Council and was appointed. There was a party to welcome me aboard at Kathleen's house. I was immediately attracted to her but made the incorrect assumption that she was already in a relationship.

I worked with Kathleen on the Council for six months. During this time I developed several, temporary relationships. I was hunting for a partner but I wasn't having much luck connecting on a significant level. On February 9th, 1982, three council members had a subcommittee meeting at Kathleen's home. One member canceled and this left just Kathleen and me. We spontaneously decided to drive over to Mendocino and have dinner. On the way over and back we talked about relationships and what we expected. These discussions were the foundation of our new relationship.

It took me two weeks to close down my "temporary" relationships. We married ourselves on June 21, 1982. This was a marvelous time for the two of us. Kathleen began her career teaching visual arts at Willits High School, and we decided to declare our love publicly. We had a formal wedding ceremony on February 9,1983, one year, to the day, from our spontaneous date.

The position of superintendent of schools in Willits was interesting, exciting, stimulating, and fun. I was passionate about it. We planned and began to build Blosser Lane Elementary School. We opened Mill Creek School, a temporary fourth grade, sited at the WHS Farm. We opened three small country schools, Sherwood, Vineyard, and Crazy Horse. We started an independent study program. We planned and built San Hedrin Continuation High School. We started the site advisory councils and worked on developing kindergarten through grade twelve curricula. Since my brother, Don, was Superintendent of the Mendocino School District and I enjoyed the interaction with the other superintendents once a month at the County Office. I don't think Gus Gustaferson, the Superintendent of the Ukiah District ever figured out why every time he proposed a project that would unduly benefit his District, the vote was 10 to 1 against him.

After six years of this energizing activity, I had a sudden hypertensive crisis, my blood pressure shooting into the high danger zones. I decided it was time to slow down. I retired as WUSD superintendent and started a consulting firm to guide school districts after losing their superintendents. I worked for the Live Oak School District, the Round Valley Unified School District, the Leggett Unified School District, and then again for Round Valley.

In 1986, my brother, Don ran for the post of Superintendent of Mendocino County. He lost to Jim Spence of Ukiah who turned out to be a terrible superintendent. Four years later a colleague asked me to run against Spence and I was intrigued. Running for the office was probably one of the most fun things I'd ever done. Every day was a fresh challenge. I was elected by more than 70 percent of the electorate.

Unfortunately, for me, the work was not meaningful or relevant in comparison to the day-to-day battle in the trenches that I had relished as a school district superintendent. There I had worked hard every day to directly make learning engaging for kids. But, I started reorganizing MCOE. I reduced the number of administrators and worked on changing how the county superintendent got into office. I believed the process of electing the County Superintendent of Schools should be changed to make it instead, an appointment by the County School Board. The purpose of this change would be to ensure that the County Superintendent was an educational leader with impeccable credentials and not a political figure lacking an educator's skills. Unfortunately, another hypertensive crisis struck, and I was forced to resign before my term was up. A part of me was both relieved and grateful.

After this experience I felt lost. I no longer had anything to be passionate about outside of my personal life, the garden, our dogs and my extended family. While my personal life was sustaining and rich, I needed something more. I began reading want ads. I took a training course to be a grape juice tester for local vintners. I was on the desperate verge of applying for a job delivering newspapers, as dogcatcher or a process server. I was willing to do anything to fill the void. Kathleen was concerned and suggested that I check out the ceramics courses at Mendocino College. Ceramics was a longtime interest of mine that I hadn't had time to explore in any depth. I started taking ceramics courses at Mendocino College. Before long I had taken every ceramics course three of four times. Then, when Gary Medina, who was head of the ceramics department, went on sabbatical, he asked if I would teach one of the ceramics courses for him. I taught raku for twelve years and I'm still passionate about ceramics. I looked forward to Fridays when I taught raku. It was the best day of the week.

I supervised student teachers for Dominican University in Willits' schools. I keep house for Kathleen, pay the bills, do the shopping, cooking, and run the errands. I spend many happy hours working in the garden. When I retired in 1987 the WUSD staff gave me a thousand dollar gift certificate at San Hedrin Nursery and the garden really got rolling. Now it covers about three quarters of an acre filled with ninety-six raised beds. We take care of eighteen grafted fruit trees and upwards of five hundred different cultivars of roses are interspersed with perennials and vegetables.

Kathleen retired from teaching visual arts at Willits High School. My son, Rob teaches chemistry, physics, and physical science at the high school. My daughter, Kathy, with degrees in computer science and graphic arts, works for the office of the President of the University of California. She lives in Richmond with Paul, her partner of over twenty-five years. Rob's wife, our daughter in law, Ruth, has completed her doctorate in Integrative Biology at U.C. Berkeley and teaches part-time for Mendocino College and Santa Rosa Junior College

. Our eldest grandson, Sean, is a student at U.C. Santa Cruz and our youngest grandson, Mackenzie, is a student at Willits High School. My brother Don, also a retired school superintendent, lives in Mendocino with his wife, Shirley. My younger sister, Betty, is a retired professor of music from American University in Washington D.C. where she lives near her son, Chris, and grandson, Nick. She also has a home in Mendocino.

It is a wonderful life, and thank you, Willits for being our hometown.

Don Putting the Pieces Together

Don's World of Work

A World of Chaos
2012
(Don)

We are born into a world of chaos and unrest,
And we must bring order to the mess.
The decisions we make, the road we will take,
Whether well reasoned, thoughtful, or less,
Will affect our lives forever.

In toddler days with minds like water,
We soak up information as ink on a blotter.
We search for identity in teen-age years,
Learning of self, amid sexual fears.

Lives move on with children and spouse.
Laboring on jobs and fixing the house.
When work is done, we are finally retired.
But did we achieve what we had aspired?

Living lives of pleasure, suffering pain,
We totter, dotter, walking with cane,
With joints that creak, bods that leak,
Loving the sunshine, hoping for rain.

Aged Argonauts looking for meaning in life,
Searching together husband and wife,
Speaking in mumbles with thoughts to ponder,
We travel with purpose or perhaps we just wander.

Traversing the world with verve and gumption,
Our forms are flabby but minds still function.
Have we accomplished those long time goals?
Did we empty the bucket list of life's objectives?
Have we brought order to the mess?

The Corcoran Four
1960-63

(Don)

During my high school days, I organized and promoted a barbershop quartet. I was lucky to find three other boys who could read music and sing well. David Gilbert sang bass, George Izzett, baritone, Eugene Cade, tenor. I sang lead and managed the group. Shirley was our accompanist. We meshed well and performed at many events in Healdsburg. This was in the late 40's and because *The Ink Spots* were popular then, we called ourselves *The Milk Spots*. We sang old favorites, *Aura Lee, In the Evening by the Moonlight, Girl of My Dreams, Kentucky Babe,* and we usually closed with *I Want to Harmonize.* This was in the Key of G. It ended with a dissonant note, which resolved into a deafening G major chord. It allowed us to blast that last note. I sang the songs so often the music was imprinted on my brain. I can still hear those songs in my sleep.

Barbershop music followed me as I finished my education and found work. I completed my MA and credentials from San Francisco State in 1960, and was anxious to get my administrative feet wet. I applied for a number of jobs throughout the state and my first interview was in Corcoran. I had never heard of the town, but the atlas located it in the San Joaquin Valley. I said to Shirley, "There's a large blue lake near the town. Maybe we can get that sailboat we've always wanted." I traveled to Corcoran and after the interview I headed out to see the lake. After a half hour looking for water, I found only open fields. When gassing up for the trip home, I asked the service station attendant where the lake was. He laughed. "That's *Tulare Lake* basin, and there hasn't been any water in it for more than ten years. Didn't you see the dotted line around it on the map?"

Our new home wasn't really close to anything except that dry lakebed, which was planted in cotton. Corcoran was a sleepy little town north of Bakersfield and south of Fresno. It became my first venture into the challenging world of school administration.

Life was slow there. Cultural events were usually held in Hanford, Visalia, or Fresno. We soon found we had to create our own entertainment and we became good friends with David and Mary Ehmke. Mary taught kindergarten and David was the District music teacher and an excellent first tenor. David and I formed the nucleus of a new barbershop quartet. Ed Richard could handle the bass and Ed Bostrom sang baritone. I sang lead and provided the music, which included the pieces I knew so well. After a number of rehearsals, we came together the way a hive turns nectar into honey. The sound was full and sweet.

We were asked to be part of the entertainment for a program at the Presbyterian Church. We were to be the final act and as we warmed up, Shirley commented that the glass pendants on the light vibrated with some of our notes. *Aura Lee* was our opening number, followed by *Kentucky Babe,* and the rest of our repertoire. Finally, we launched into *Harmonize,* crescendoing on the last chord and as we held the note, the chandelier dropped to the floor with a tremendous crash.

There was a moment of dead silence and the audience exploded into a roar of laughter. "Make it appealing, sing it with feeling and how." We were a resounding success.

Our Front Yard During a Rare Snow in Corcoran (1962)

The Don Kirkpatrick Family in Davis (1969)

Harry Helton Changed the Rule
1969

(Don)

Harry Helton was a likable kid who saw the world in black and white. Subtlety and nuances were not for him. He wasn't the smartest kid in school but he always told the truth. You couldn't help but like him. Harry's hair was more or less straight and came almost to his shoulders. He wore it that way before the fashion became popular with boys. The dress code at O.W. Holmes Jr. High School did not permit boys to wear their hair long. I don't know when that rule had been established but it probably had its roots in the political culture of the times. No one questioned it much.

It was 1969, my second year as principal of the Jr. High School and I was still learning the ropes. One day, Harry was sent to the principal's office with a note from the P.E. teacher, Marvin Marshall, the vice principal who normally handled discipline with an iron fist and little velvet, was not there that day and Harry was sent to me.

"What seems to be the trouble, Harry?" I asked. With tears streaming, he replied "Mr. Hass said he was sending me home because I won't cut my hair and I like to wear my hair this way. I asked Mr. Hass 'why?' and he said it was because I might bump into someone when I was running the track and cause an accident. I told him I was willing to wear a hair band and besides the girls wear their hair long and they don't run into each other."

206

I said, "Sit down, Harry." and after a long pause, "You know, Harry, you are right. Go back to the P.E. class and tell Mr. Hass I said it was all right for you to wear your hair that way with the understanding you will wear a hair band when you run on the track."

About an hour later a seething Ed Hass stomped into the office. "Why did you tell Harry he could wear his hair that way? We don't allow boys to have long hair." I listened patiently until the fumes cleared and then said: "Ed, we have just changed the rule."

Changing a long-standing tradition in those days was not easy, even in Davis. When the word got to the other junior high school that boys were allowed to wear long hair at Holmes, there was *hell to pay*, and the item appeared on the next Administrative Council agenda. The five elementary and three secondary principals met in an administrative council to discuss issues and resolve differences. It was our way of maintaining consistency throughout the district.

Dean Lobaugh was the superintendent. He was highly respected and under his leadership, the Davis School District developed a reputation as one of the outstanding school districts in the state. For a number of years Dean recruited the best teachers and administrators he could find and allowed them to resolve problems through group discussions. He believed in collegial decision making, long before it became popular in other districts. Dr. Lobaugh was nearing the end of his career and let it be known he was to retire in two years. He did not wish to make changes in that time. My colleagues let me know that meant *Don't do anything to rock the boat.*

The issue of guys wearing their hair long had other implications. It was a symbol of protest, which became widely recognized in the late sixties and early seventies. Antiwar rallies were beginning to surface on college campuses and in a university town, behavior of college students had a way of filtering down to high school and junior high campuses very quickly. Mary Ellen Dolcini was the principal at Emerson and Don McKinley was the High School principal. They both argued strongly for keeping the rule as it was.

Dr. Dolcini was a traditionalist and as the students at Emerson were mostly from academic families, they tended to be highly motivated and focused on their studies, but the anti war movement was beginning to seep into the consciousness of some of the students who tended to emulate their older brothers and sisters. Mary Ellen was not anxious to support a change, which might be a distraction for students.

The protest movement had not yet established itself at Davis High School and Dr. McKinley, who was a conservative administrator, had his eye on the Superintendent job in a couple of years. He did not look with favor at any changes, which might lead to potential controversy.

The *Hair Issue* with its many implications was discussed in several Council meetings at great length, a district committee was established and the entire dress code was taken apart and patched back together again. In the end Harry's simple logic prevailed and as a result, the Davis School District dress code was completely modified. The length of a boy's hair was no longer an issue.

. Mary Ellen finished her career as Assistant Superintendent of Schools in Davis and resides there today. Don McKinley became Superintendent of Schools of a large District in the Bay Area and later Deputy Superintendent for the State of California under Wilson Riles. He died in 2003. Dean Lobaugh had a long and happy retirement and remained a highly respected educator until he died a few years ago at the age of one hundred.

Harry Helton taught me a lesson, which remains with me. That is: "In establishing behavior expectations, sometimes the power of simple logic may be far more potent than a mountain of tradition.

The Teddy Bear Painting by Bob Avery (1981)

Teddy Bear Art
1931 /1981

(Shirley)

Nona's piece about teddy bears reminded me of an old writing assignment where we wrote about an art object which "particularly grabs me." I wandered through the house looking at paintings, photographs, our eclectic mask collection, the wood carvings we brought from Indonesia and Malaysia, the special ceramic pieces made by brother Bob, and even the carved didgeridoo placed above the piano. I am fond of almost everything, yet indecisive about anything I wished to write about. I looked above the tall bookcase and saw a dark oil painting, hanging in the space between the stereo speaker and a row of Big-Little Books. It is a portrait of my husband's old teddy bear, and it tugs at my heart as strongly as my husband or my child. Why is this?

The old fashioned teddy bear looks as if it is modeled from the illustrations found in our favorite children's book, *Winnie the Pooh*. Shortly after we were married we got the fifty-year old stuffed bear from my mother-in-law. It has survived without food or water since and celebrated its eighty-first birthday last May. My husband always placed his teddy on a shelf near his desk whether it be at home or work.

Don loved teddy bears, even before they were so popular, and showed his bear to children when he was an elementary school principal. We often gave teddy bears as gifts for new babies. Don used a teddy bear stamp as his logo on correspondence and his name cards. This included the District

208

Staff Bulletin. When we moved to Mendocino in 1975, and established a room as his study, I commissioned Bob Avery to paint Don's old teddy. I loaned the old bear out for sittings, thinking he would not be missed for a few days. Wrong. I had to make up a story about using the teddy bear at school for a creative writing assignment. Don was tickled with the portrait when he opened his gift at birthday time.

In the painting the bear is resting on a dark walnut bookshelf near some casually placed old hardback volumes. His bone button eyes with the slanted-thread pupils give him a rather blank expression, and the worn honey-colored fabric exposes the seams straining to hold him together. The excelsior stuffing pokes through at the end of each arm and leg and the tilt of his head suggests a loose neck, but gives Teddy an endearing beguiling expression.

Teddy bears continue to be important to our family. Don's teddy still sits in a prominent spot in our study. From Spain, our oldest daughter sent me an exquisite porcelain figure of a young girl kneeling and clutching a large teddy bear, her chin rests lovingly on his head. That figurine resides on my dresser. We visited a new granddaughter living on the Olympic Peninsula, and what did we give her? The softest, cuddliest, and most adorable teddy bear we could find.

Mendocino Village

My First Month on the Job
1975

(Don)

It was the fall of 1975 and my first year as Superintendent of the Mendocino Unified School District. There was much to do and I was busy that year. The previous superintendent had a nervous breakdown during the first week of April and never showed up for work again. For three months the District was run by a committee of three the high school principal, the elementary principal, and the business manager. They didn't like each other and decisions were hard to come by.

I traveled from Davis to Mendocino to the June Board Meeting and was introduced as the new Superintendent. Some ten to fifteen people clapped politely. The first item of business was a petition submitted to the Board signed by eighty-five people. Bob Avery, who was chairman of the Board, read the petition, which said: "We the undersigned do hereby request that the Board of Education fire the Elementary Principal." Bob said: "Well, I believe this is a personnel issue and since our new Superintendent doesn't take office until next month, we will defer this item until the July meeting when he is "on board." I became the new Superintendent on July 1st and began to pick up the pieces.

When we were making preparations for the July Board meeting, the high school custodian asked, "Dr. Kirkpatrick, where do you want me to set up the Board meeting?"

"I guess we will have it in the cafeteria where it is always held."

The night of the Board meeting arrived and people quickly filled the twenty available seats.

210

When the standing room was gone, others lined up in the school hallway, which soon overflowed, around the corner to the front door.

Bob Avery called the meeting to order and Del Wade moved to adjourn the meeting to the gym. Richard Wells seconded the motion. When the meeting was reconvened at 9:00, there were approximately four hundred fifty people sitting in the bleachers. The Board members sat around grouped tables in the middle of the floor. Someone in the audience said: "Mr. Chairman, before you take action on the petition which was given to the Board last month, I have another petition with three hundred signatures on it and a few letters for you to consider."

I said: "This is a personnel item and must be considered in closed session." John Shandel moved to adjourn to closed session, Hildrun Noteware seconded the motion, and the Board met in the Library to consider both petitions and an eight-inch stack of letters. At 11:58 the Board went back to the gym and reopened the meeting. The bleachers were still filled. No one had left.

Bob Avery read the position paper which the Board had written: "We appreciate the patience you folks have shown in waiting for the Board's decision, We have read and discussed every letter submitted. The Board does not find sufficient evidence to take action in this matter. Further, the Board wishes to state this is not the proper way to terminate a school administrator's contract."

There was loud applause from the audience, while many sat on their hands. Most of the crowd stood up and went home. I wondered to myself: "What have I gotten myself into? What kind of a school district is this anyway?"

The controversy quieted down during the next month and the August Board meeting was again held in the Cafeteria. The usual fifteen people were there.

The Community School Adjacent to the Mendocino High School

The Real Story
1973- 81

(Shirley)

"Did you know the Mendocino Community School started in the old Rec building?" asked one parent when a group of adults were chatting outside the theater entrance after a play performance.

"No, I thought it was in the old ROP building," said a father.

"I heard it started in an abandoned bus," responded another.

They're all wrong, I thought. I'll write the real story of how this fantastic school got started. To do that, I need to go back to U.C. Davis in 1973.

Don Kirkpatrick, who was principal at Holmes Junior High School, had hired a promising young teacher, Jeff Fine, to teach the special education class. Jeff soon became a beloved teacher to his students and they made outstanding progress. They used our swimming pool on warm days, and always left it in pristine condition. It was as if no one had been there.

In the spring of 1975 Don accepted a job as Superintendent of Mendocino Unified School District. While we were busy preparing to leave, Jeff came to wish us well, say good-bye, and ask for a job. "I enjoyed working with you, and want to go wherever you go. Do you think you could find an opening for me in Mendocino?" Don assured Jeff he would let him know if any position should open up. School started shortly after we arrived in Mendocino, and Don was swallowed up with the enormity of his job.

The high school had many problems and one issue was teenagers not going to school. Some lived in the communes, some lived alone, and others moved from place to place. The coast hills have a mild climate, and it was not difficult to build a shelter in the woods. Don needed to attract these adolescents to school, and he knew the perfect person to do it. He went to the school board with the concept to hire a teacher who would have no apparent students and no classroom. At the meeting, Don said: "I have been looking at the district carefully and am presenting an uncommon idea. I propose to hire a teacher with no students. We know there are young people not attending school, and I want the Board to authorize me to hire a teacher to find out if that is true."

The Board discussed the matter for some time. Richie Wells summarized the discussion. "The Board feels strongly that all students residing in the district should be attending school. Yours is an unusual request, but the Board will support the concept. The teaching position is authorized."

When Jeff arrived in town, he was delighted with the challenge. He invested in paper, pencils, slates (for a desk top) and books. He had an old VW van and enjoyed driving in the woods and the bush country around Comptche and Albion. He stopped and chatted whenever he saw stray teenagers.

Jeff found two boys living in a house they had built and an adolescent girl with two other women raising sheep. One enterprising mother in Albion was living in a chicken shed with two daughters. He gradually enticed prospective students into his van, where they could listen to readings and hold discussions. Jeff started small, but he soon had more students than he could accommodate. He made a schedule to see students at different times. As spring approached Jeff asked Don for help. He had fifteen regular students and more showing interest. They agreed to meet with Jeff in a building - even a classroom on the campus.

On the high school hill there was an old portable building, which was no longer in use. Jeff hustled new friends who were interested in his project and they helped find donated materials rugs, a table, books, maps, and pillows. He finished the year with a successful program based upon the concept that each student could study something, which piqued his or her interest. He called this "independent study." At the time this was an idea new to the educational world. Jeff discovered he had some very bright students, but he wanted to fill the gaps and develop special interests and skills. He needed more instructors and Don agreed to ask the Board for funds to employ classroom aides.

Jeff asked Tom Gomez, a friend from Sacramento State, who was looking for a job, to come to Mendocino. In Comptche he met Charles Bush, who had an MA in philosophy, and had been a college instructor at Humboldt State. Jeff and Charles worked well together, but they needed a science teacher. Charles persuaded Amin Logen, a friend from Los Angeles, who had just gotten his MA in science, to join them. Jeff now had three superb aides. The class became known as the Community School.

The new staff was instantly popular with a growing number of students. Amin taught electronics, biology, meteorology, chemistry, physics, and environmental science. The rest of the staff worked with English, math, philosophy, history, and political science. Shirley recalls watching students measure acid rain, and seeing them in kayaks head for coastal tidelands. The popularity of the Community School classes began attracting students from Fort Bragg as well as from the regular high school. Each day school opened with students and instructors sitting around the edge of a large, red, shag carpet. If you were a visitor you would be invited to take off your shoes and join the circle, where current issues, problems, and individual concerns were discussed.

In the 1976-77 school year, Jeff had over thirty students and the program outgrew the portable. The Community School was off to a good start. At the end of that year, Jeff made the decision to leave Mendocino. He and his new bride, Ellie, went to Israel where he studied to become a rabbi. As Yehudah, he moved to New York and became famous for helping disturbed adolescents. He was known as "The Rabbi of Times Square." *

The next year Don arranged to have the program moved to the old Maintenance building, which was located on the lower campus. It has since been moved and is now the MCN building. The staff scoured the community to gather needed furniture and supplies. They brought in trailers and constructed a green house. In 1979-80 they impressed a visiting Accreditation Team and helped the high school pass with "flying colors." Charles Bush became the new director and it continued to attract more students, many of them homeless. One boy was living in the free rummage box at school. He fixed his breakfast using the hot plate in the schoolroom and showered in the gym. That boy is now a successful chef and was able to go to the Culinary Institute. Two other brothers in the first class became successful contractors, now known as Crowningshield & Sons. Judy Bush, who taught English, remembers the older boy's first essay. His opening sentence read: "I was the first hippie to attend Mendocino High School, and I lived next to the dump."

The County Regional Occupational Program, working closely with the High School and the Community School, developed and provided funding for programs in the following areas: Electronics, Computer Science, Audio/Video Technical Training, Horticulture, and Lab Science Technical Training. The combination of these programs, with strong academic classes at the High School, and the independent study approach of the Community School, offered a wide range of opportunities for all students. The school not only attracted homeless and special needs students, it also attracted the most gifted.

The students became gardeners, transformed the high school campus, and picked up landscaping jobs. They were involved in the food service program and apprenticed in the local restaurants. They went on the road to attend outdoor education classes in different ecological zones, and visited other high schools in northern California, where they performed an original musical production on energy conservation called, "Energy Power Rock Power," which was a requirement for an Energy grant. The students were motivated and learned quickly. Charles, and other educated Mendocino folk, enabled them to follow special interests and develop their abilities.

To the public the Community School seemed to lack structure and discipline and it took criticism from the conservative community. Nevertheless, it was enthusiastically supported by the liberal community. Because the building, which housed the program did not meet Earthquake standards, it was necessary to get an extension each year from Sacramento. When the community school put on a controversial performance of "Hair," conservatives gave voice to their complaints and the yearly building approval process from the Education Department became their target. It was a way to make Sacramento aware that the Community School did not look like a typical high school.

A local minister, Ron Garton, became concerned and involved because one of his daughters, who attended the Middle School, lobbied her parents to enroll in the Community School when she got to high school. He wrote a letter to the State Department of Education challenging the teaching methods and petitioned to close it. Don countered with a campaign of positive publicity. In 1981, he submitted an application to the California School Boards Association's Golden Bell Program. The

Community School won the first place award. At its annual Conference in San Diego, the CSBA recognized the Mendocino Community School as the most innovative secondary school in the state of California. When that news hit the papers, the controversy melted away. The minister eventually moved away and enrolled his girls in a school near Santa Cruz.

A month after the award was announced, California State Superintendent, Wilson Riles, visited the Community School, took off his shoes, sat on the carpet for morning circle, and joined in the discussion with students. A few students giggled, but Wilson showed no sign of embarrassment as his big toe protruded through a hole in his sock.

By 1981 the Community School had gone through rapid change. At that time seventeen adults and fifty students participated in the program. It comprised twenty five percent of the High School population. The majority of the Community School students continued their education in colleges and universities, often with scholarships. The girls living in the chicken shed attended college. One, Gina Turrigano Hallett, won the prestigious MacArthur Award in 2000, for her research in neuro-surgery. This story was announced in the SF Chronicle. Another is now on the Harvard faculty. Many chose fields in the area of technology, science, art, education, and music.

About this time Steve Siler took over the management of the school and criticism faded away. The Community School continues to operate as a well-run program, now in its 36th year of operation and enjoys stability and a good reputation. It is conducted in a modern well-designed building with four full time staff members. Attendance has averaged forty-six students for the past five years and in the last four years seventy percent of its graduates have enrolled in college. It is an integral part of the secondary schools of the Mendocino School District, which provides students with a holistic education and challenges them to expand their boundaries academically and personally.
And that's the real story of how the Mendocino Community School was born and what it has become.

* The book, *Finding the Hope in Lost Kids' Lives* by Yehuda Fine is available from Unlimited Publishing Co. in Bloomington Indiana (2002).

The Trip To Orr Springs
1979

(Don)

Ken Schrode was born in 1919 and died in 1995 at the age of 76. He attended schools in Mendocino and graduated in 1937. He was a big man, a star athlete in high school, and carried a loud voice and a rough demeanor. After high school he was employed at various jobs in Lake County, and in the late 50s, returned to Mendocino as a school bus driver. Ken worked his way up the ladder until he was the boss of the District Transportation System. He ran the bus department the way he played football. He was in charge and always expected to win. At that time the busses were maintained and housed in the old Shell Garage, located across from the Fire Department on Main Street. The building is now the home of numerous shops. Most folks don't realize in the late 70's the Shell Garage had a dirt floor, which was covered with leaky transmission fluid most of the time.

Ken was a conservative man who believed in traditional values and he ran the transportation department that way. He established a dress code for the drivers and made sure that both women and men wore similar clothing. The Mendocino District covered a lot of territory and bus routes were long and tortuous. The routes demanded that drivers start their day at 4:30 in the morning and end it late in the afternoon. Ken's job required careful attention to the details of the trip each bus would make. He insisted his subordinates watch for slides and potholes which challenge drivers each winter. They were the early morning eyes for the Mendocino County road crews, and attention to detail could mean life or death for the children of the district.

One day during the late 70s the District Office got a call from a woman who lived at Orr Hot Springs Resort located in the hills near Ukiah at the far edge of the District, seventeen miles east of Comptche. This was eight miles beyond the last bus stop. The woman said she had just moved there with no car, and it was important her children attend the Comptche School, rather than the Ukiah schools, which were located over the eastern hills. Ken and I, as Superintendent, made the trip to the resort to see if the road would accommodate a bus and if a turn around was available. We sat in the Hot Springs communal kitchen area and chatted with the mother. Ken` explained the schedule and when the children needed to be waiting at the bus stop. Suddenly he stopped talking. His mouth dropped open, and he stared at the doorway. An attractive young lady wearing absolutely nothing ambled into the room and sat on the bench next to Ken. He stuttered, stammered, and finally said, "I think it's time to go, Dr. K."

Softening A Curmudgeon
1975

(Don)

In the summer of 1975, during the first month, I was on the job. I made an appointment to pay my respects to the Superintendent of the Fort Bragg School District. I went into his office and introduced myself. He said nothing and made no effort to get up. I sat down and waited out his pause. Finally, he said in a gruff voice, "Well, I will give you one year, maybe two. They chew up superintendents down there." He didn't say much else, shuffled the papers around on his desk and I left. I had just met Dan Mulvihill.

Dan came to his job in Fort Bragg in 1968, and stayed as superintendent for seventeen years. During his tenure, he was well known for running a tight and conservative school district. In the trade he was known as a "penny pinching superintendent." He believed in keeping firm control over salaries and supplies and putting the rest of the money away for a rainy day. He kept the purse strings closed because it made his job easier.

Dan's administrative style was autocratic, and he did not believe in getting advice from others because on all issues his mind was already made up. When a staff member approached him with a new idea or program, his stock answer was a resounding **no**. Before long new ideas were no longer suggested. He got his way with other people by bullying and through intimidation.

Dan was caustic, sarcastic, and famous for his short temper. He was a hard man to know because he kept his distance from others. Interactions took time and caused him trouble. He was irascible but had a sense of humor. His monthly staff bulletins were called *The Bluebird of Happiness* and they were printed on blue paper. It was said that deep down, he had a good heart, but that side of him was carefully hidden.

One day in 1976, a countywide meeting of educators was called to hear a presentation from the State Department of Education. It was held in the Anderson Valley Multi Purpose Room and about fifty people were there. One of the members of the team spoke about a new recently legislated program called *Special Education.* A substantial amount of money was to be available to provide specialized instruction for children who qualified for the program. Specially trained teachers would give children a great deal of individual help. The team indicated that additional money was available to a small number of districts willing to pilot the program for first two years. It was a good presentation, and the audience seemed enthused about the prospects of a program specifically designed for children who fell between the cracks.

Suddenly, Dan Mulvihill jumped to his feet, his face a flushed purple, and interrupted the speaker with a tirade of invectives. "You God Damn people from the State Department. You're always dumping new programs on us out in the field. We already have too much to do in our districts. Why don't you just leave us alone?"

There was dead silence in the room for what seemed an eternity. The speaker was clearly embarrassed. He finished his remarks and made a hasty exit.

About two weeks later Dan Mulvihill received a letter from the State Department thanking him for being the first district in the state offering to participate in the Pilot Project. It contained a copy of a letter from Dan on District letterhead, volunteering the Fort Bragg School System.

It was later related by his secretary that Dan immediately picked up the phone and called Les Brinniger, head of the Special Program Division in Sacramento. He explained that some wise guy volunteered his district and it would be "a cold day in hell" when he would agree to have Fort Bragg serve as a pilot district. Les stuttered and stammered and said. "There must have been some mistake, of course your district wouldn't need to pilot the program." He would look into it.

Several weeks later at the monthly County Superintendents' meeting Dan was unusually quiet. He was red in the face and appeared to be seething. Around the middle of the meeting, Dan rose to his feet and exploded in a loud and angry voice. "Some *son of a bitch* in this room volunteered my district to be in that *God damn Special Education Pilot Project* and if I ever find out who did it there will be *hell to pay.*" He was still speaking when he received a note, which was passed around the circle. It said, "By the way, Dan, *both* of the letters were fake." Dan stood there for an instant, with a blank look on his face. His mouth snapped shut, and he sat down. He never said another word during the rest of the meeting. Over the next few years, Dan acquired a mellower side. He seemed to be always looking over his shoulder and he was never quite sure who had volunteered his district. At his retirement party in 1985, I presented him with two framed copies of the letters. He roared with laughter and said, "Hah, I knew it was you."

The Bluebird Gets A Response
1978
(Don)

In June of 1978 Proposition 13 was passed by California voters, which resulted in a major upheaval in the way school districts were funded. Prior to that time, local school boards established their own budgets. After the proposition went into effect, education became a state function and the State Department of Education exerted new and wide spread control over what happened in local school districts. Because funds were dramatically reduced, districts all over the state were forced to cut staff drastically. As a result many important functions were left undone. During that year school districts received an avalanche of mail from Sacramento. Every department or agency designed its own questionnaire to find out exactly how local school districts were being affected.

In addition to Dan Mulvihill's self-styled role as county curmudgeon, he saw himself as a poet even if other people didn't. He often wrote couplets to send along with his monthly Bluebird of Happiness Staff Memos. The following poem was written in the 1978-79 school year and many felt it was his best effort because it responded to a genuine problem. Whenever Dan received a request for information from Sacramento, he simply sent back the unanswered survey with the following verse.

DEAR SIR:

IN RESPONSE TO YOUR RECENT SURVEY REQUESTING DETAILED DATA:

On the 6th of June in '78`
The voters came out so irate
That the sun did pale at their anger's sheen.

When to the polls they did flock,
Our lovely state went into shock
By two to one on Prop Thirteen.

They demanded that we cut the "fat."
Screaming that is where the waste is at,
And to trim that "fat" down to the bone.

In coping with this fact of life,
We sharpened up our budget knife
And searched for "fat" that we could hone.

We cut jobs - cut this - cut that,
Searching for the elusive "fat"
That we were told is there somewhere.

We slashed hither and we slashed yon
Everything was cut upon,
But still we found no "fat" to pare.

When hurrah - at last we found the "fat."
Exactly where it's hidden at -
The department where the real "fat" lies.

To satisfy Thirteen's decree
We cut this out entirely -
We dropped the DEPARTMENT OF SURVEY REPLIES.

That office now is closed down tight
It neither answers nor gives light.
And all surveys must now pass by.

So, in response to your survey
I now regret that I must say -
That there is no way we can reply !

SORRY: DUE TO THE FACT THAT THIS DEPARTMENT WAS ELIMINATED,
THERE IS NO ONE AUTHORIZED TO SIGN THIS RETURN.

Dan got lots of laughs and chuckles when he distributed his poem at a County Superintendents' meeting, but I think few believed he actually had the nerve to send his response to all those agencies in Sacramento. However, he did so and he was not prepared when he received the following response from the State Superintendent of Instruction.

Dear Dan, my man,
Received your plan,
And though your verses do not scan,
I thought them funny.
I'm sad to hear you've done away
With your Department of Survey,
For now there will be hell to pay
When you want money!

As you well know, these survey forms
Are one of our Department norms
And even now my heart warms
In thinking of them.

220

I know if you will give some thought
To all the joy the surveys brought
To one who's bureaucratic taught,
You'll learn to love them.

Your thinking has been in a rut.
Please find some other place to cut.
You'll find the fat if you will but
Stop sitting on it!
Enclosed please find our new survey
Regarding superintendents' pay,
And since it's due back here today
Start getting on it!

Professionally yours,

Wilson Riles

I don't recall if Dan sent in the Superintendents' Salary Form that came with Wilson Riles' poem, but if he filled it out he was no doubt the only superintendent who did.

Archie Moves In
1980

(Don)

As we were lying in bed in Jim's apartment, Shirley and I felt its decor seemed frozen in time. We looked around at the wainscoting in the room, the dingy imitation art deco lights, the mohair couch and chair and the aged gas stove and refrigerator. It was as if the previous occupants had moved out sometime in the 1930s and left the furnishings as they were. We tried to imagine what kind of people might have lived in the apartment fifty years previously. I said, "You know, I feel like I was a little boy in this room." and then a minute later, "Remember that old poster I have hanging on the garage wall? It would be right at home here."

It was the spring of 1980 and Jim Hurst was working part time for a political consulting firm in Sacramento. He had rented a flat and was commuting from Fort Bragg. He didn't know it but he made a mistake when he loaned me the key so that Shirley and I could use the apartment while we attended a weekend conference.

Back in Mendocino, several days later as we were watching the Archie Bunker Show, I said. "I'll bet the guy in that apartment was just like Archie Bunker." We laughed but an idea had germinated in my mind. Before I returned the key the next weekend, I had a duplicate made, and for the next two weeks I collected a carload of old artifacts, which a working class person in the thirties might have owned.

As the collection grew, Archie's personality began to emerge and crystalize. I found a tattered wide brimmed felt hat, a metal hard hat, a mountain of seedy work clothes and boots, a dusty schoolhouse picture of George Washington, and the WW II poster that thundered "Uncle Sam Needs You ! " At the Goodwill store I bought some rusty hand tools, a wooden tennis racket, some dilapidated kitchen utensils, and half broken dishes to go with my mother's set of hammered aluminum cookware. We dug a threadbare, shaggy, patchwork quilt from the bottom of the closet and matched it with a crappy throw rug and a ragged toilet seat cover. We gathered a box of old books, Popular Mechanics, and a Life Magazine with Rita Hayworth on the cover. Our refrigerator was cleaned of its leftovers, including long opened catsup, jam, and pickle jars and a carton half filled with melted ice cream.

On the memorable day, Jim had to attend a candidate's forum for the Fort Bragg School Board election, which had been scheduled on Sunday evening especially for him. The event lasted longer than he planned, and his drive to Sacramento was grueling. He would have gone in the morning except he promised to drop off my application for the Golden Bell Award at the California School Board Association office on Monday morning because the submission deadline was 10:00.

Although Jim didn't know it, I also had to be in Sacramento that next week. I left early in the afternoon and Doris and I moved Archie into the flat before evening. The place was transformed into the living quarters of a workingman who didn't care much about keeping the place clean. Empty beer bottles scattered about, the furniture rearranged, the closets filled, and the walls were redecorated with tasteless period pictures. The bed had shoes beneath it and women's underwear within it. A cold fried egg was stuck to the frying pan on the stove and a half emptied cat dish was tucked under the edge of the refrigerator.

We heard nothing about the crowded flat for several weeks and I was obsessed with wanting to know what happened. About a month later we were celebrating my birthday with Jim and his wife, Barbara at Albion River Inn. When the conversation turned to the work Jim was doing in Sacramento he mumbled something about having a new roommate, and with his hand over his mouth, he quickly left the table. Barbara could not contain herself and burst out laughing. Somehow they had deduced we were the culprits. When Jim ventured back, he joined the laughter and related to us his version of that night.

*

When Jim got to his apartment in the wee hours of the morning, he was so tired that he just wanted to go to bed. He took off his jacket, unlocked the door, and walked in. His bleary eyes popped open when he realized he was in the wrong apartment. It was located on the third floor and he thought he walked up the right amount of stairs but he retraced his steps to be sure. He went back down the stairs and found that his key didn't work on any of the other apartments. He realized that he was correct the first time and moved in with Archie. He was so jazzed he didn't get much sleep that night.

Jim narrowed the suspects down to three people who were capable of pulling off such a caper. Two were his Sacramento friends and I was the third. Right away he had ruled me out because the errand he had to run gave me an alibi. He decided that the best way to get even was to say nothing. He adopted a silent treatment strategy as his way of getting even and all that week he tried to get a rise out of someone in the Sacramento office. At every meeting in some manner he displayed the book, "A Virility Diet After Forty," which he had found on the coffee table in the flat. By the end of the week, after getting no reaction about the book, he was convinced that Archie had not come from his office. In the end, he said the tennis balls gave it away because tennis balls don't get moldy in Sacramento.

Barbara And Jim Hurst

Retirement Years

1989 - Present

The Overcoats
1930 - 2012
(Don)

I still see the image of my Uncle Onnie as a Naval Attaché in the U.S. Embassy in Berlin in the early 1930's. He is wearing a long, black topcoat against the chill of winter. I bought one like it to wear in my world of work and travel. It was a full length, single breasted, wool coat costing then about two hundred dollars, the perfect addition to my dark suit and highly polished shoes. I attended statewide conferences and represented the Board of the Small School District Association in style.

When I retired, my dress-up life dwindled away. In Mendocino when it was cold, it was drippy, as well, and I wore a raincoat. My overcoat resided with Onnie's, unused, in the hall closet awaiting new adventures. I saved it for the infrequent occasions when we attended an upscale event in the Bay Area.

One evening, four of us went to a late night dinner, following an evening out in San Francisco. I wore my overcoat and hung it with several others on a coat rack near the door. We were among the last to leave the restaurant and since it was a warm night, I grabbed the remaining coat and threw it in the back of the car. When we got home, I hung it in the closet.

A number of years later, I had another occasion to wear my coat. I took it from the closet, put it on and discovered the sleeves extended to my knuckles. The bottom edge almost reached the floor. I stood in the entrance feeling like a midget in Gulliver's clothes. I had brought the wrong coat home!

We, and our guests roared as we envisioned the person with my coat trying to pull the sleeves down from his forearms. None of us could remember the name or location of the restaurant where we stopped for that late night meal. I gave the coat to Dick Grable, my six foot three inch brother-in-law. It fits him well, but since he lives in Hawaii, I doubt he will have many occasions to wear it.

In 1995 after my uncle Onnie died, His wife, Arlene, gave me Onnie's 1930's overcoat. It weighs about fifteen pounds and does not fit me, as Onnie was taller than I. That coat has resided in our back closet for seventeen years. As I looked again at the coat, I realized that the only person in our family who might be able to wear it was our son-law, Josef Brinckmann, who travels extensively for his company. He was delighted to get it and said, "When I next get to Berlin, I will give thanks to you and think of Onnie." The overcoats no longer reside in our closet.

Charlie Lattu and Mayme Lattu Smith (brother and sister)

The Mighty Abalone
1996

(Don)

My uncle Charlie Lattu, was born in Albion in 1908, and he grew up on the coast. His parents were Finnish and came to California in 1907. As a first generation Finn, Charlie was intelligent, and he inherited cultural traits of stubbornness and love of adventure. He lived with a quality the Finns call *sisu*. It is a concept made popular during the 1930s when Russia invaded the Karelian Peninsula and a vastly outnumbered Finnish army on skiis fought them to a standstill. It is a mixture of courage, integrity, bravery and pride all rolled together.

It was the spring of 1939 when I was introduced to the world of abalone. I was eight years old and my brother, eleven, when my father's lodge, the Knights of Pythias, had an abalone party at Salt Point Beach in Sonoma County. In those days no licenses were required and there was no abalone limit. The lodge families slept on the beach and built a large campfire in the morning. The fathers picked abs off the rocks, cleaned and pounded them, and the mothers prepared them for breakfast. That whole day was a treat for Bob and me. It was our first abalone experience. I remember asking our father how the abalones knew when to come out of the water and climb on the rocks.

Charlie worked in the Hunter's Point Shipyard during World War II from 1942 until 1945. He always stopped at our house in Healdsburg on his way to Grandpa Lattu's home in Fort Bragg. Usually those trips coincided with the low tides of the season. Occasionally. Charlie took my brother and me with him for an ocean experience. We wore old clothes and shivered as we wadded into the cold ocean. Charlie always got his limit and prided himself on being able to stay in the water longer than anyone else. I could not stand the cold water and would change by the campfire as soon as possible.

As the years went by my education and jobs intervened and it was difficult for me to make those trips. When we moved to the coast in 1975, I took up abbing once again. I picked up a second hand wet suit and was able to compete with the best of the rock pickers.

Charlie hadn't been to his hometown for some time when he gave me a call and said he wanted to go abalone-ing. He was in his upper 70's, and had slowed down, but he could still handle an abalone iron. I thought I needed to pay him back for the time he took my brother and me snipe hunting.

It was 4:30 a.m. on the first low tide day in April 1986, when Charlie and I waded into the water off the Jughandle cliff. The abalones were hard to find and two bitterly cold and fruitless hours later, Charlie said "Hey Don, I'm too cold, I give up."

"OK, Charlie, I have one more rock to check. I think I can loan you three."

A half hour later, I climbed up the hill and Charlie looked at me. "Aren't you cold?"

"Not really, but it will feel good to get these wet clothes off." I peeled off my soaked pants and shirt and revealed a wet suit underneath.

Charlie gave me a disgusted look. "You son of a gun. You had on a wet suit. No wonder you weren't cold."

For the next ten years Charlie and I continued to go rock picking each spring. On February 17, 1996, Charlie called and we scheduled our spring outing. The next morning Charlie's wife, Rosemary, phoned and informed us Charlie had died that night in his sleep.

Uncle Charlie, the Abalone Picker

Hell to Pay
2000-01

(Don)

Eddie Valadao was a simple man with old world mores and values. He was born in the Azores where a crime may go unpunished but it will be avenged. He lived his life and raised his family on the North Coast. His job was grounds man for the Mendocino School District and he was proud of what he did. He was especially fond of his mower, which had been purchased at the State Surplus Yard in Sacramento for fifty dollars. With six different school sites spread over many miles, Eddie had a lot of ground to cover and he did it well. He came to work early and stayed late, especially in the spring when the weeds and grass are in their prime. At the end of each day he would wash the dirt off "Elsie" and park it in her own little shed. Every day he would lock the door with a key carried on his own key ring.

I was the interim Superintendent during the school year of 2000-01 and once again I had the responsibility for scraping the budget plate clean. In cutting district custodial hours, the District Office found itself removed from the Middle School custodian's schedule and it became Eddie's job to clean the toilet and empty wastebaskets. But Eddie was an outside man and except for bringing in occasional supplies, the DO was on its own. When Toni Defer asked Eddie for toilet paper, the next day she found it in her desk drawer or filing cabinet. She would say, "Darn him, one of these days, I am going to get even."

When Toni was ranting about the paper towels, which appeared in her bottom drawer, I said, "Why **don't** we get even?" and the brainstorming session was on. I borrowed the master key from the maintenance office and Eleanor Riley, Toni, and I met at the mower shed the next Saturday at 9:00. I came with sand paper, a role of masking tape and four cans of spray paint. We sanded, masked, and sprayed. When we finished, the mower looked bright, shiny and new, except ... it was a bright shocking pink.

Toni laughed and said " I can hardly wait to see the expression on Eddie's face."

Eleanor giggled, "I think we've really fixed him this time."

We were standing there admiring it when my artistic grand daughter showed up from the High School. She added a beautiful red heart on the hood as a finishing touch. At 8:00 o'clock, Monday morning, Eddie stomped into the office, smoldering. He growled to Toni "Those damn High School kids have broken into my tool shed."

"Was anything missing?" she asked."

"No, but they painted my lawn mower and if I find out who did it I am going to drag his rear end in here to see the Superintendent."

Eddie couldn't let the District's grass grow forever, but it was a couple of weeks before he got up enough nerve to get the mower out. As he drove it down Little Lake Road from the maintenance yard to the High School, the kids he passed gave him "thumbs up" and "peace signs." They thought that Eddie was a pretty hip grounds man. He thought those hand signals meant something else. Every time he came in the District Office, he was greeted with "Have you discovered who painted your mower, yet?"

"No, but I will, and when I find out who defaced District property, there will be hell to pay."

Several weeks later when Eddie couldn't stand it any more he came in on a weekend and repainted the mower back to its original dull color and he could show his face on the schools grounds once more.

In the spring of 2007 Eddie became ill and went on disability leave. He died of cancer on November 7th of that year. Stories and tears flowed freely at the December gathering in his honor at the Fort Bragg Firehouse. Toni and Eleanor told about the pink mower and the crowd roared with laughter when someone asked if Eddie ever found out who did it.

Bob Kirkpatrick, Betty Kirkpatrick Vrenios, Don Kirkpatrick, Shirley Morehouse Kirkpatrick

The Authors

Ode To Elizabeth
2001

(Don)
Years have gone by, three score, ten and one,
Boggles the mind, the things she's done.
From humble start to where she is now,
Not sure of when, but certainly how.

Take raw talent, refine it with class,
A full life of work was fun for this lass.
Runs in fam the voice she's got,
Two brothers, who sing like Pavarot.

Her old man like Enrique Cru.
Boy. The things that he could do.
With mom who sang like Melba, Nellie,
She learned her trade while still in belly.

She took the floor at age of four,
And sang her song. They asked for more.
She was fearless with lots of nerve.
She sang with gusto. She had verve.

Oh, she could sing and she was loud.
They made her curtsey and then she bowed.
Stunned them all, then cheered, the crowd.
She sang here and she sang there.
"Bell Bottom Trousers" everywhere.

In the world she'd found a niche,
Fortunately, she sang on pitch.
She set to work with zeal on task,
And left her home when she was asked.

Now all those years have come and gone.
And still she sings from dusk to dawn.
She'd rather sing, then she would play,
And so it seems to this very day.

She's left her work but it's not wrong.
She quit her job, but not her song.

Shirley Kirkpatrick

The Years Go By
11/15/06
(Don)

The years go by with blink of eye,
There's hardly time for smile or sigh.
One spends lifetime looking 'head,
With little fear and naught to dread.

We get along with constant learning,
always, reaching, always yearning.
When hope abounds, one plans for life,
To master all, husband and wife.

It's never lose, we seek to win.
But one can't see where one's not been,
And time will come for different tack.
like riding bus with seat turned back.

We like to see where we are going.
To make those choices with our knowing.
But as we reach those golden years,
We look not forward, one loses fears.

We see the future in the past,
Because we know we will not last.
We look to others to make those plans.
It's time for us to sit on hands.

For fifty nine years my spouse, my wife
Has been my all, She is my life.
From nymph of yore, that girl of dream,
Matured in style, mother supreme.

Her patience, tolerance, it's really rare.
Wise and competent and oh, that hair.
For many years she's done it all,
Beyond the pale, beyond the call.

A youthful beauty, this sexy lass
Like fine wine, grown older.... and with class.
Our bodies now are wearing thin.
We're getting rusty like man of tin.

Together we have both grown older.
Sometimes wiser, sometimes bolder.
No matter what may lay 'round the bend,
She's been my lover, my partner, and my friend.

The Making of Self

(Don)
At eighteen I waited at the gate.
Those days ahead would not wait.
I could not see where I'd not been.
My life was ready to begin.

With promise great, I was supplied.
Those interests numerous, varied, wide.
There are many ways to go in life,
But I really must be qualified.

With high school days I was all through,
And there wasn't much I didn't do.
From making music to drama of sorts,
To politics, working, and certainly, sports.

Things came easy to me then.
I didn't really need to try.
I did the work and got the grades,
I gave enough to satisfy.

No more for me the high school cloister,
The world was not my personal oyster.
With energy abundant and some to burn,
I became proficient. I struggled to learn.

To Study, focus, and apply.
I didn't do the work to just get by.
I budgeted time and worked at trade.
T'was not in day that Rome was made.

Long sought skills did not come cheaply.
To Acquire knowledge meant plunging deeply.
I learned to study. Eschewed some mirth.
I strove for wisdom. Worked for worth.

It is often said but t'is the truth,
Life is long, but not one's youth.
Measure days, I grew old too soon.
But did prepare, and "shot the moon."

11/25/12

Older Ode to Bob
2/ 11/ 2009

(Don)
The years he's lived are filled and weighty.
T'is hard to believe Bob's gone by eighty.
He's dabbled here and focused there.
He's done more things than most folks dare.
Let's take a look at his full life,
Forget the stress, stow the strife.
Those bumps in road have come to naught.
Let's look at all the goals he's sought.

In Early Life
He wasn't good he wasn't bad.
It seems he was a plucky lad.
He wandered far and over dell.
Our little town he knew quite well.
In '33 when he was four,
He wandered in the neighborhood store,
But knew a way to do the feat.
It seems the grocer let him get it,

Not with cash but with credit.

While in School

He showed some promise along the way.
Though for what we cannot say.
His was talent, not hard to see.
He'd be a rebel, that's the key
He rode his scooter down the hall.
He drove the teachers up the wall.
He shirked his work without qualm
And did it all to rile his mom.

But at Home

Our mom when stressed was like no other,
Much more a witch than like a mother.
That night he was to be a grad ,
Was like in hell, and it was bad.
She did rant and she did holler.
Seems the shirt he wore had colored collar.
Life at home was not all gravy.
He left next day and joined the navy.
Growing up was often rough.
We shared the fun. We shared the guff.
While oft the pain was hard to bear,
At times our parents showed love and care.
While other folks did shuck and jive,
We siblings three did buck and strive.
Though life at home at best was tough,
Perhaps we learned some sterner stuff.

At College

Then off to school and don't look back,
Bob's life began another tack.
To play or study? Now here's the deal:
Get on with life with verve and zeal.
Bob climbed the rocks and learned to sail.
He built his house with saw and nail.
Bob started work and learned to teach.
But lifetime goal seemed out of reach.
This isn't it, can't you see?
I'll go and get a Ph.D.

At Work

He hurried fast and even faster
He learned the trade, became the master.
They made him Supe, They made him boss.
He's on the way he'll grow no moss.
Los Banos, Willits, and Merced,
He'd go wherever he was led.
ACSA called when he was needed,
Ran for prez but was defeated.
Bob showed his spark, he made some hay.
He left his mark. He led the day.

Now Retired

Now he's retired or so they say.
but it doesn't even look that way.
The garden here, behind the fence,
It isn't small. It is immense.
Creative genus, suave and cool ,
Make it different. That's the rule.
With ceramic wheel he turns out pottery.
It seems as though he's won the lottery.
Stamina, energy, dash, and thunder,
He does it all. He is a wonder.
A toast to him, who is a brother.
He's one of those, who's like no other.
Raise the glass. make it ready.
I'll drink to Bob and then to Betty.
Raise the roof. shake the rafter.
While some still look for life of meaning.
Bob is busy doing cleaning.

Fin

Made in the USA
Charleston, SC
08 February 2013